mission-shaped
youth

mission-shaped
youth

rethinking young people and church

Tim Sudworth
with Graham Cray and Chris Russell

CHURCH HOUSE
PUBLISHING

Church House Publishing
Church House
Great Smith Street
London SW1P 3NZ

Tel: 020 7898 1451
Fax: 020 7898 1449

ISBN 978-0-7151-4082-6

Published 2007 by Church House Publishing

Printed in England by the Creative Print and Design Group, Blaina, Wales

Contents

Series introduction

In adopting and commending the *Mission-shaped Church* report, the Church of England took an important step forward in its understanding of God's mission. It is a journey full of opportunities and challenges, and one which opens up new questions. This series of titles is designed to resource thinking, reflection and action as the journey continues.

Each title in the *Mission-shaped* series considers how the principles presented in *Mission-shaped Church* can be applied in different areas of the Church's life and mission – in work with children and young people, in rural areas, in the parish church and in the area of apostolic spirituality. What perspectives and inner values are necessary to be part of a mission-shaped Church today? These areas were touched upon in the MSC report but are now explored in more depth.

All the authors write with the benefit of years of practical experience. The real-life case studies and practical examples they provide are designed both to be inspirational models of ministry and mission and to be adapted by the reader for their own context.

The examples cited include both 'fresh expressions', developed as a response to the culture of a particular group of people, and more traditional models, reflecting the fact that 'there are many ways in which the reality of "church" can exist'.[1] This series is firmly committed to advocating a mixed economy model for the Church of the future.

[1]Archbishop Rowan Williams, from the Foreword to *Mission-shaped Church*.

Acknowledgements

This book could not have been written without the support of colleagues and friends who also share a passion for God, Church and young people. To all the people who sent contributions for this book a big thank you, and special thanks go out to those people who still serve God's kingdom and young people on a weekly basis through groups, open clubs, schools and congregations – may many be added to your tribe.

Tim Sudworth would like to dedicate this book to Nicki, Jake, Ben, Dan and Jas.

The publishers would like to thank Jenny Baker and Georgia Litherland for editorial assistance.

The authors

Tim Sudworth is Diocesan Youth Adviser in Guildford Diocese. He has worked in a variety of youth ministry positions in various parishes since 1993. He is currently training as an Ordained Pioneer Minister through St Paul's Theological Centre in London.

Graham Cray is Bishop of Maidstone and the Bishop for Mission in the Diocese of Canterbury. He was previously principal of Ridley Hall, Cambridge. He chaired the working party that wrote *Mission-shaped Church* and was part of the working party that produced *Youth a Part*. He has recently contributed to the Church House Publishing titles *Making Sense of Generation Y: The world view of 15- to 25-year-olds* and *The Future of the Parish System*. He is also chairman of the Soul Survivor Trust.

Chris Russell is proud to call Reading his home. Married to the universally popular Belinda, father to three daughters, since 2001 he has been vicar of St Laurence, a church that meets in a reordered twelfth-century building in the centre of the town. They see themselves as a parish church for the young people of Reading, a vocation that is stretching, exhilarating and far more difficult than any of them ever grasped. Chris previously worked for Soul Survivor, Watford, and as a parliamentary researcher.

Foreword

How far we have come in a generation! When I was ordained just over twenty-five years ago, 'youth work' in the average parish was relegated to the young curate whether he had the talent for it or not! Taking place at a safe distance from the regular worshipping congregation, they generally lamented his failure to 'get them in' but in reality would have been quite incapable of responding positively to the implications of a group of teenagers arriving for morning service!

Ferret through the divine encounters in the Gospels and you will discover that it was the startling willingness of Jesus to meet, speak and eat with just about anybody; the feeling he engendered that they could dare come to him as they were, that transformed them. That beautiful 'acceptance in their unacceptability' brought about repentance, forgiveness and the discovery of the joy that life with Jesus brings.

The truth is that, often without realizing it, the Church does just the opposite. It requires people to change *first*, to be other than they are *in order* to hear God's word and receive the sacraments, or even just to belong – especially young people, who often have to become 'old'.

And yet, young people are often the most mission-shaped Christians! Their seriousness, their energy and their joy are a leaven God wants in his world. To listen to the unselfconscious testimonies of teenagers before they are fully immersed in the fiery waters of baptism, knowing that a good number of their unconverted and wondering friends are in the Assembly because they have been invited to witness the encounter, rebukes my timidity every time. To share in risky worship that allows transitory and, yes, sometimes tawdry youth culture to rub shoulders with the inevitably stronger abiding Tradition of Word and Sacrament is to have your faith in the power and love of Christ renewed.

This book is full of wisdom and experience. I hope it will engender a new courage and a new generosity to re-make our structures and worship opportunities so as to gather up young people 'that none be lost'. The need is urgent!

+ Lindsay Urwin OGS

Bishop of Horsham

Introduction

Tim Sudworth

As I was writing and researching this book I was privileged to be invited to speak to one of the youth congregations that is featured later. As I sat at the back thinking holy thoughts and preparing myself to deliver what I thought God wanted to say to these young people I overheard a conversation between a group of young people operating an audio-visual system. These two speakers were part of a larger group who sat around a sound desk and a bank of computers, totally focused on delivering a well-managed and slick service. It was clear that they had a strong sense of belonging in this setting and the conversation went as follows:

> Young Person 1: 'That's the problem with education isn't it?'
> (The whole group leans in and one person responds)
> Young Person 2: 'What is?'
> (at this point I'm intrigued and lean in also)
> Young Person 1: 'Giving knowledge to idiots'. (agreeing nods all round)

Now I'm not going to judge what that young person said, but I am using the story to illustrate a unique situation that happens when young people are allowed to be involved in and be part of Church. In this particular congregation we saw operating a beautiful example of the kingdom of God. The more musically minded young person would find a role, the more hospitable would find a role and, yes, the slightly nerdy would find a role – and within all this they could feel accepted, loved, valued and challenged for who they were – *without the risk of being labelled a failure*. Where else in our communities should our young people be valued and

The stories in this book reflect a church where young people are valued, loved, accepted and safe. What greater mission can there be than to provide a safe, loving, accepting and challenging environment for the young people of all our parishes?

loved for everything they can be and everything they are? Where else in our communities should our young people be allowed to explore fundamental questions of existence without the risk of being judged or labelled a 'pass' or 'fail'?

If nothing else many of the stories in this book reflect a church where young people are valued, loved, accepted and safe. What greater mission can there be than to provide a safe, loving, accepting and challenging environment for the young people of all our parishes?

The purpose of *Mission-shaped youth*

The major part of this book consists of stories of people and projects that are responding to that call to mission. They give a window into some of what is happening around England and the Scottish Borders at the moment. The stories describe a diversity of situations and ways of responding to them, but throughout I discovered one consistent element – the undying commitment of a few passionate, godly people, both working with young people and empowering work among them for the sake of the kingdom of God, creating those safe, loving, accepting and challenging environments. This book is dedicated to those people who endure nights of worry, planning programmes, finding new volunteers and having to explain the latest breakage in the church hall to the PCC. These people are saints in every way.

Some of the projects described in this book may be short-lived fireworks, but they blaze a trail of change and influence in their churches and localities. Others may be more long-lasting and evolve into maturity. These projects are offered to inspire and encourage others wondering how to reach and work with young people who inhabit a markedly different culture to that of the mainstream Church. They also offer us much to reflect upon and learn from. In Part One of the book, Bishop Graham Cray, chair of the group that produced the *Mission-shaped Church* report, reflects on the 'mission-shaped' values of youth ministry.[1] In Part Three, we draw on the case studies presented in Part Two to offer some challenges and encouragement to the wider Church.

However, this book is not an attempt to prescribe one model or even a set of models for work with young people. As the Church of England report, *Mission-shaped Church*, so clearly explained, there is no 'one size fits all' model. In Archbishop Rowan Williams' memorable phrase, we need to move towards a more 'mixed economy' – 'recognizing church where it appears and having the willingness and skill to work with it'.[2]

Churches seeking to reach out to and nurture young people need to be aware of the culture in which they live and move and have their being (to paraphrase Paul in the book of Acts). In Acts 19 we read about Paul going to Ephesus. When he started his ministry there he preached to the Jews in the synagogue and, to put it bluntly, he got nowhere. So after three months he found a neutral place, the hall of Tyrannus, and preached to everyone, Jews and Gentiles alike.

Paul tried a model he knew, found it didn't work, looked at the culture and environment he lived in and adapted his strategy. He didn't expect the Gentiles to come into the alien environment of a synagogue; he went to them. So in Chapter 3 you will find a brief description of the world that young people are growing up in today. The case studies in Part Two (Chapters 4, 5, 6 and 7) show that each work with young people is unique, because it develops according to the needs of a particular context and, more importantly, the young people in it. The case studies show the importance of prayerfully and wisely discerning two things when you begin work in a particular area: the needs of the young people, and what you believe God has in mind for the area and the group he has called you to work with. In order to help you think through how you can develop such a vision, questions for reflection and discussion are included at the end of each section.

The case studies also highlight the many challenges which people encountered in implementing their vision – the familiar challenges of proper resourcing and of dealing with opposition, often from those who might have been expected to be most supportive. The implications of these challenges for the wider Church will be considered in Chapter 9. But first let's define some words to save confusion later.

Where does the term 'mission-shaped' come from?

The Church of England report *Mission-shaped Church* was published in 2004. It was produced by a working group of the Mission and Public Affairs division, under the chairmanship of Graham Cray, Bishop of Maidstone. To the surprise and delight of all those involved, the report has attracted a huge level of interest in the Anglican Church and beyond.

What is a 'fresh expression'?

Mission-shaped Church included many examples of new ways of being church, which it termed 'fresh expressions'. In his presentation of the report to Synod, Bishop Graham explained the use of this term:

> The strength of 'fresh expressions' was the direct connection to the Declaration of Assent: the faith 'which the church is called upon to proclaim afresh in each generation.' Our findings show that the challenge to proclaim afresh is no longer primarily a matter of the faithful translation and communication of the gospel but also concerns the very shape of the local church itself.[3]

As a result of *Mission-shaped Church*, a new Archbishops' initiative called Fresh Expressions was set up in 2004, working across the whole of the Anglican and Methodist Churches to resource and encourage new ways of being church. Steven Croft is Archbishops' Missioner and team leader of Fresh Expressions. He sees fresh expressions of church working alongside traditional local churches in the new 'mixed economy'.

> We need fresh expressions of church in order to engage effectively with the more than 60 per cent of the population who are beyond the reach of traditional local churches. Establishing fresh expressions of church demands a willingness for the church culture to be shaped to some degree by the culture it is trying to reach. It also demands a willingness to listen to the Spirit in each place to discern the right starting place and way forward: there can be no blueprint ... A fresh expression of church is not normally seen just as an additional activity or simply a stepping stone for people to come to Sunday services but as something with the potential to be or become church for those who take part.[4]

The current working definition of a 'fresh expression' (as used in the May 2006 Fresh Expressions prospectus) is as follows:

- A fresh expression is a form of church for our changing culture established primarily for the benefit of people who are not yet members of any church.

- It will come into being through the principles of listening, service, incarnational mission and making disciples.

- It will have the potential to become a mature expression of church shaped by the gospel and the enduring marks of the church and for its cultural context.[5]

A note on the terms 'youth work' and 'youth ministry'

Over the last couple of years there has been a lot of debate, and some feel confusion, about what is going on in youth work / youth ministry / Church-based youth work / youth work and ministry. Some use the words interchangeably. However, in recent years, others have used the term 'youth ministry' to define a distinctively Christian approach to work with young people (the term 'youth work' can cover both secular and Christian contexts). Pete Ward defines youth ministry thus: 'Youth Ministry in this sense is an attempt to express that there is an approach to youth work which operates within a different code to that developed within secular youth work which is nevertheless also professional.'[6]

Graham Cray further explores the particular values of youth ministry in Chapter 2 of this book and throughout we have tended to use the term 'youth ministry' rather than 'youth work' to avoid confusion and hopefully set the benchmarks of a distinctive approach.

Questions for discussion

1. In what ways are you able to create an environment where young people are safe, loved, accepted, challenged and valued?

2. Should the priority of the church be to look after the young people that we already have, or to reach out to young people outside? Which are we better at doing? Where should we be putting our resources?

3. Can a church do both – nurture its young people *and* reach out? If so, how?

4. Do we really want young people as part of our church?

Part One

Mission-shaped youth
Where are we now and how did we get here?

In Chapter 1, Tim Sudworth gives a brief history of youth work and youth ministry, by way of setting the scene for where youth ministry has come from and where it may be going ultimately. In Chapter 2, Bishop Graham Cray explores a fresh theology of youth ministry, proposing five 'mission-shaped values' that may serve as cornerstone of the future work of the Church with youth. Then in Chapter 3, Tim Sudworth explores the world of young people – the creativity, the passion , but at the same time the dark side of youth culture.

How did we get here? A short history of youth work

Tim Sudworth

Youth work, and youth ministry for that matter, is not a new thing. We may sincerely believe that we have created innovative ways of working with young people, but this is not usually true. In many ways, the Fresh Expressions definition of a fresh expression of church simply describes what the Church has needed to do through the ages: to adapt to the surrounding culture and to communicate in ways that people can understand. Likewise, if we look back at the history of youth work in this country we'll realize that most of our 'new and improved' youth-work projects and methods owe more to our predecessors than we give them credit for. As a wise man once said, there really is 'nothing new under the sun' (Ecclesiastes 1.9)!

> ❝If we look back at the history of youth work in this country we'll realize that most of our 'new and improved' youth-work projects and methods owe more to our predecessors than we give them credit for.❞

A few years ago I was in a second-hand bookshop, having a good rummage around for some holiday reading. My wife closely monitors the books that I take away with me and any which include the words 'Youth', 'Ministry', 'Theology' or 'Church' in the title do not pass the test. One that slipped through, however, was the wonderfully titled *How to Work with Lads* by Peter Green, published in 1929. I discovered that Canon Peter Green was a vicar in Manchester and had previously worked in Leeds. His work in Manchester ultimately saw him receive the Freedom of the City of Salford in 1944. Many of the strategies he outlines in his book would easily fall into the category of a fresh expression of church, focusing on the many people who lived in his parish but who weren't going to church.

This book woke me up to the extraordinary inheritance of ministry among young people that we have in the Anglican and the wider Church community, going back over two centuries. To truly understand where we are now we first must understand our inheritance and history in youth work (and ministry).

The early pioneers

There is a certain amount of debate as to who should suffer under the title of First Recorded Youth Worker. Brierley firmly drapes the mantle on the shoulders of Hannah More.[1] Hannah was greatly challenged by the work of William Wilberforce and his determination to improve the lives of the poor. Two years after first meeting him, Hannah and her sister, Martha, set up their first Sunday school, in which they used a simple programme of basic education, alongside religious instruction and vocational training. Sunday schools had been around since the seventeenth century, but what was distinctive about Hannah and Martha's school was their pedagogy, the range of activities they included and their ability to inspire others to do something similar. Over the next ten years they set up a further twelve of these Sunday schools.

Robert Raikes might also be regarded as a pioneer in this field. In 1780 he set up a 'school for the children of chimney sweeps' in Gloucester, which was quickly replicated in other areas. By 1784 there were an estimated 1,800 pupils in Sunday schools in northern cities; some were even attended by adults. By 1851 three-quarters of working-class children were attending many different types of Sunday school with varying emphases on formal education, religious instruction and social justice.[2]

The year 1844 saw the establishment of the Young Men's Christian Association (YMCA) by George Williams in St Paul's churchyard in London, in order to 'enable working young men to come together for prayer, Bible study and to win others to Christ'.[3] During the Victorian period we also see the increased use of the word 'youth' as a recognized category, with its own needs, influences and stages of development. In the 1880s and 1890s youth work with more of an emphasis on justice rather than an evangelical focus began to spring up. A lot of these projects focused on areas of injustice among young people, particularly among young women in the work place.

The twentieth century

The period after World War One saw the beginning of state involvement in youth work. This was mainly due to a massive postwar increase in youth crime. Even though the government instigated the setting up of local juvenile organizations that included committees to coordinate and focus youth provision, youth work was always going to be the poor cousin of formal education and so missed out on funding and Parliamentary focus. It still is, and still does.

The period after World War Two brought clearer aims for youth work, which focused on 'physical and social training'. By 1948 an estimated 1,800 full-time youth leaders were employed, the majority through voluntary organizations.[4]

In the 1950s there was a diversion of funding from youth work into the Welfare State. As a result, the number of full-time youth workers declined drastically until it was approximately halved. In 1960 the statutory Youth Service came into its own, with the publication of the Albemarle Report. This report was a massive breakthrough, which led to youth work being officially recognized as a form of education in its own right. This led to a significant increase in provision for young people in youth clubs, and just as importantly, the youth worker became a professional. By the end of the 1960s the numbers of youth workers were back up to pre-1950s levels.

Church youth work: the 'safe alternative'?

In the 1960s church youth groups positioned themselves as safe alternatives to the changing and often frightening (for the church) youth culture that was growing around them. Both Ward and Brierley describe the 1970s as a period when the Christian youth scene built on this idea of safe alternatives.[5] The Jesus Movement incorporated the musical style and feel of the youth culture that surrounded it: 'Whilst youth subcultures were experimenting with drugs, Christian young people were discovering the power of the Holy Spirit.'[6]

As time went on the gap between secular youth work (with a focus around the National Occupational Standards for Youth Work set by the government) and youth ministry (with a distinctively Christian focus on mission and discipleship) began to get wider. The Church of England designated the 1990s as a 'decade of evangelism'. At this point, the Church's aims and goals were clearly at odds with those of secular youth work. The 1980s and 1990s saw a massive increase in the number of youth workers employed by churches. However, only secular organizations offered professionally recognized training. Even the training provided by organizations like the YMCA did little to develop youth ministry as a distinct discipline involving theology as much as youth-work practice.

> **The 1980s and 1990s saw a massive increase in the number of youth workers employed by churches.**

This situation changed in the 1990s when distinctively Christian youth-work training courses were developed. The Centre for Youth Ministry and Oasis were among those who began to create and provide training and resources in Christian youth work and ministry. These courses sought to unify the best of both worlds, by combining the JNC, the main secular youth-work qualification, with a healthy understanding of a practical theology.

> **Informal research suggests that nationally the number of youth workers employed in churches far outnumbers those employed by local councils.**

Some people have said we now have a situation that has 'parallel but overlapping disciplines of "youth ministry" and "youth and community work"'. Informal research suggests that nationally the number of youth workers employed in churches far outnumbers those employed by local councils, and yet many government initiatives fail to recognize the quality, quantity and drive of church-based youth work.

Questions for discussion

1. Who are the significant people who have helped you in your journey of faith? Why do you remember them and what have they contributed to your life? In particular, and if appropriate, consider those who were formative in your childhood and teenage years. What would you like to say to them now?

2. How has your church's ministry to young people changed in the last 10, 20, 30 or even 50 years?

3. How well resourced is your youth ministry – in terms of money, people and the value it has within the church? What resources do you most lack? What can you do about it?

4. Has the professionalization of youth ministry been a good thing for the Church? Think through the pros and cons.

5. Do we really want young people as part of our church? How might this question have been answered at different stages in the last 200 years?

2 The seven mission-shaped values of youth ministry

Graham Cray

As Tim Sudworth has alluded to in Chapter 1, the last two decades of the twentieth century provoked a serious re-evaluation of youth ministry. Both the English Churches Survey and the survey commissioned for the Church of England report *Youth A Part* 1996 confirmed that during that period the number of young people up to 19 in church had halved.[1] The rate of decline was faster among teenagers than among most other age groups and clearly required careful analysis.

The Church's work with young people always gives advance warning of changes which will impact the whole of culture. But it became clear that young people were on the leading edge of a very substantial cultural change.[2] They are, as it were, the first settlers in a much changed world. Douglas Rushkoff wrote, 'Without having migrated an inch we have none the less traveled further than any generation in history.'[3] It was an obvious exaggeration, but was not totally misleading. In their review of sociological studies of youth in the UK, Furlong and Cartmel reported that 'Young people today are growing up in a different world to that experienced by previous generations', because they are 'subject to uncertainties which were not part of day to day life for previous generations'.[4]

In his analysis of recent church growth and decline, Archdeacon Bob Jackson has written,

> The Church's work with young people always gives advance warning of changes which will impact the whole of culture. But it became clear that young people were on the leading edge of a very substantial cultural change.

7

If the decline of the Church is ultimately caused neither by the irrelevance of Jesus, nor by the indifference of the community, but by the Church's failure to respond fast enough to an evolving culture, to a changing spiritual climate, and to the promptings of the Holy Spirit, then that decline can be addressed by the repentance of the Church. For true repentance involves turning around and living in a new way in the future. A diocese or parish, which, out of repentance, grows a new relevance to the contemporary world, may also grow in numbers and strength, because the Spirit of Jesus has been released to do his work.[5]

This clearly applies to youth ministry as much as to any other aspect of the Church's mission, but what would be the appropriate 'new way' of working?

Within the Evangelical tradition of the Church, in particular, a substantial transformation has taken place. Some longstanding youth ministry organizations, such as British Youth for Christ and Crusaders, have effectively reinvented themselves. Others have faded away or amalgamated with larger groups.[6] New organizations, like Soul Survivor and the Message Trust, have come into existence.

As a consequence, youth ministry, in the Evangelical wing of the Church at least, is being understood differently and practised differently. The purpose of this chapter is to outline some of the distinctives of this approach.

The missiology of youth ministry

Perhaps the most important change of theological perception was the identifying of youth ministry as a missiological task, rather than primarily as a pastoral or educational one. In what we might call a Christendom context,[7] the Church's work with young people could assume a general knowledge of the Christian faith, a strong Christian influence in culture, and reasonable parental support for its work. This was embodied in the placing of national, and many diocesan, youth and children's departments within boards of education.

None of this remains the case in a post-Christendom context, where most young people are substantially ignorant of the Christian faith,[8] where young people are the generation with the lowest percentage for belief in God,[9] and where the churches compete for prime time on Sunday mornings with a wide range of leisure activities, and parents no longer believe that their children 'ought' to go to Sunday school. Youth ministry is essentially a missiological challenge, which includes education and pastoral care. This argument was laid out

> ❝Youth ministry is essentially a missiological challenge, which includes education and pastoral care.❞

in the theological section of *Youth A Part*[10] and related directly to the wide ecumenical theological consensus which saw mission as sharing in the mission of God.

Pete Ward, then the Archbishop of Canterbury's Advisor on Youth Ministry, developed this further.

> The Christian gospel tells the story of a missionary God. Relationship is at the centre of the being of the God whom we know as Father, Son and Holy Spirit. We see the God who is three and who is one as he is revealed in mission. We know of God in no other way than as one who seeks humanity in relationship. It is this God who calls us and inspires us to reach out to young people. Youth ministry or Christian youth work is therefore grounded in the missionary nature of God. The mission is God's not ours. We are called and inspired by God to participate in his seeking of relationship with all human beings.[11]

Any approach rooted in the mission of God must come to terms with the Incarnation. At its heart, the shape of the mission of God is that the Father sent the Son in the power of the Spirit. 'Consequently, if the church is to carry out its commission faithfully, it must draw its models, inspiration, motivation and wisdom from the earthly ministry of Jesus in relation to his Father and the Holy Spirit.'[12] This emphasis on the Incarnation[13] opened up a rich resource of contextual theology and inculturation theory, which could be applied to youth ministry. Youth ministry was 'mission in the context of culture'.[14] The disciplines of sociology and cultural studies provided tools and insights for the analysis of youth cultures and of their relationship to the overarching culture of contemporary Britain. Missiology provided new tools for engagement. Youth ministry often pioneers new insights and good practice for the whole Church.

> **Youth ministry often pioneers new insights and good practice for the whole Church.**

The theological emphasis of *Youth A Part* actually anticipated the main themes of *Mission-shaped Church* by eight years.[15] Some of the main headings of the theology section, that youth work is incarnational, relational, a call to discipleship, and community building directly anticipate *Mission-shaped Church*'s five marks of a missionary church. *Youth A Part* mentions the new phenomenon of youth congregations and also addresses 'alternative worship'. These were both in the list of emerging forms of church which the *Mission-shaped Church* working party was asked to address.

Inevitably there was a dialectical relationship between the establishment of new practices on the ground and the new sources of theological reflection. Each informed the other, as a new praxis emerged.

Marks of youth ministry: a new paradigm

Through both trial and error on the ground and missiological study, a new paradigm for youth ministry emerged during the 1990s. As with all paradigm changes, the new model contained many features which had also belonged to the old. It was evolution rather than revolution, but a new model was needed for a new time.

The essential features of the model are as follows:

1. Youth ministry is relational.

2. Youth ministry is incarnational.

3. Youth ministry recognizes the priority of worship.

4. Youth ministry relies on the transforming power of God.

5. Youth ministry recognizes that mission is holistic.

6. Youth ministry is a long-term process.

7. Youth ministry recognizes the importance of discipleship.

We will now explore these features of youth ministry in greater depth.

1   Youth ministry is relational

One of the first key expressions in the new paradigm of youth ministry was 'relational youth work'. Youth work has always centred on building trusting relationships with young people, but the emphasis in a Christendom context was often on educational programmes. In a model with a relational emphasis programmes continue to have their place, but are subordinate to relationships. Education in the faith remains critically important, but good relationships create the environment where an appetite for learning can be developed and sustained. 'Relationships are the only means we have of enabling and encouraging young people to reach maturity in their physical, emotional, social and spiritual lives.'[16]

> **In a model with a relational emphasis programmes continue to have their place, but are subordinate to relationships. Education in the faith remains critically important, but good relationships create the environment where an appetite for learning can be developed and sustained.**

It is important to note that this is a value for youth work, that it will aim to build and develop community among young people, as well as between young people and youth workers. It has at times been misunderstood as a pressure upon youth workers to spend an unrealistic proportion of time developing and maintaining an unsustainable number of personal relationships with young people. Such criticisms are entirely fair.[17] Youth workers will need to model costly relationships, but the purpose is the creation of a community where each has friends and each is treated with dignity.

2   Youth ministry is incarnational

Helmut Thielicke once remarked that, 'The Gospel must be constantly forwarded to a new address because the recipient is repeatedly changing his place of residence.'[18] Youth ministry has always needed to keep in touch with trends in youth culture, if only as a matter of respect for young people and to show an interest in their interests. But the current transitions are not so much in youth cultures, which are always changing, but a substantial transition in

> Youth ministry has become a matter of cross-cultural mission. It involves entering the young people's world and honouring them by taking it as seriously as they do. The aim is to help them to find Christ there, and to equip them to be agents of his kingdom, where they are, from day to day.

Western culture as a whole.[19] On the whole we are not dealing with temporary subcultures, which young people can be expected to grow out of; we are dealing with the culture in which they will grow up. Youth ministry has become a matter of cross-cultural mission. It involves entering the young people's world and honouring them by taking it as seriously as they do. The aim is to help them to find Christ there, and to equip them to be agents of his kingdom, where they are, from day to day. This does not involve any pretence at being trendy, but it does involve a willingness to lay aside one's own preferences and accompany them in the opportunities, joys and sorrows they face. It is in their world they have to be Christians, and we need to take care that the environment we create equips them to serve Christ in their world, rather than deskills them.

3   Youth ministry recognizes the priority of worship

Contemporary youth ministries whose priority is the leading of young people to faith in Christ see worship as their primary value. This is a theological conviction, a conviction that worship is the first and primary vocation of all Christians, which needs to be learned early. This does not mean that all evangelism is done by drawing young people into worship events; often this will not be appropriate. But it does mean that a primary object of youth ministry is the winning of worshippers. Worship, and music in worship in particular, is a key aspect of inculturation. For many young people this is found in the soft rock worship style, which has an international appeal. In fact youth ministry provides many of the songs loved by adults. Matt Redman, Tim Hughes, Martin Smith and other songwriters all developed their art within youth ministry, and continue to be involved in youth events. For more urban young people Hip Hop, RnB and Gospel may well be more appropriate. Others are profoundly moved by the music of Taizé. What matters is that the music is culturally appropriate. Culturally appropriate music in worship is central to the forming of a group or congregational identity. It acts as the cultural glue which holds a youth ministry together and keeps it missiologically relevant.

Creative approaches to prayer are also important. The 24-7 prayer movement (featured in Chapter 7)[20] has integrated the evangelical tradition of intercessory prayer with many practices of prayer from the ancient church. Prayer stations and prayer rooms are increasingly common as young people are learning to pray with faith, imagination and all their senses.

4 Youth ministry relies on the transforming power of God

At the heart of this approach to youth ministry is a belief in the transforming power of God and the gospel. Encounter *with* God, not just belief *about* God, is central. This may be through charismatic encounter or contemplation, but it is all about a God who can be known and experienced. God through Christ has the power to save, bringing young people into the assurance of salvation. The same God has the power to heal, and to transform lives and communities. Young people are not interested in a God who makes no difference and no demands.

> "God through Christ has the power to save, bringing young people into the assurance of salvation. The same God has the power to heal, and to transform lives and communities. Young people are not interested in a God who makes no difference and no demands."

This requires a balanced diet of word and Spirit. The Bible will be central to youth ministry, and youth leaders will need to assume major if not total ignorance of it, the more they engage with unchurched young people (the great majority). However, the Bible is the menu not the meal. It is intended to lead people into the experience of the things it teaches. Every Christian needs personal experience of the inner witness and the power of the Holy Spirit. Young people are no exception.

> **❝** Youth ministry is less about ministering to young people and much more about equipping young people to exercise ministry. **❞**

Through the gospel God not only saves, but commissions and equips for service. Youth ministry is less about ministering to young people and much more about equipping young people to exercise ministry. It is about empowerment in Christ. After years of involvement in the Church's work among young people my greatest regret is the low level of expectation I had had of them, not individually, but generically, as demonstrated by the models of ministry we were using. We were educators (telling them what they ought to know), entertainers (keeping them happy, so they didn't get bored and leave) and police (protecting the church premises from them, and them from the world outside.) Education still matters, and youth ministry should be both joyful and safe, but our task is to equip them to change their world in the power of Christ.

Empowering and equipping young people to take responsibility for their own ministries involves mentoring, it involves enabling them to receive the gifts of the Spirit. Good practice these days includes peer-led youth cells and youth worship bands. It also involves mission, by young people, not only to other young people, but to the wider community.

5   Youth ministry recognizes that mission is holistic

Good practice in mission is holistic. Holistic (or integral) mission integrates evangelism, the healing ministry in all its dimensions, and service to the community. 'Words, works and wonders'[21] belong together. Young people are the best evangelists to young people, and equipping Christian young people with the skills to be witnesses to their friends is a core activity. At the Soul Survivor festivals, some years ago, we disbanded our prayer ministry team and replaced it with a team of coaches ('enablers') so that we could teach the young people to pray for one another, for healing and other needs. Expectant faith is at the heart of faithful discipleship and need be neither triumphalistic nor naive.

Young people grow in faith, or into faith, when given the opportunity to engage in holistic mission. 'Not yet' Christians see the relevance of the faith as they join their Christian friends in service to the community. Christian young people learn the need to be good news if they are going to share good news. Many youth groups now practise what is sometimes known as 'servant evangelism'. Young people from deprived areas are empowered to be a positive influence in their own communities. More affluent young people begin to learn to serve, and are introduced to the biblical priority for the poor.

The emphasis is on the long-term transformation of communities. Soul Survivor's involvement in The Message in Manchester (2000) and Soul in the City in London (2004) proved transformative for many young people, and contributed to long-term change, including crime reduction, in a number of communities.[22] The long-term Eden Project developed by the Message Trust in Manchester as a key component of their evangelistic work in urban estates has provided inspiration for a number of other cities.[23] An annual coordinated weekend, The Noise, provides the structure for youth groups to serve locally, but together, every Mayday Bank Holiday.

There are dangers, as well as strict health and safety procedures, in all of this. Projects must genuinely be for the sake of the local community, not just to purge middle-class consciences. Programmes must be from and with the local community, not directed at, or merely for, them. What is intended is the development of a way of life, not just the social concern branch of a youth programme.

6 Youth ministry is a long-term process

The core aim of Christian youth ministry is to enable young people to become life-long followers of Jesus Christ – to find salvation in him and give themselves to serve in the kingdom of God. This is a long-term process, irrespective of how the young people come to or express Christian commitment. With an increasing number of young people we are starting with almost complete ignorance of the Christian faith. We start a long way back and should expect it to take time. Nothing

> With an increasing number of young people we are starting with almost complete ignorance of the Christian faith. We start a long way back and should expect it to take time.

15

attracts young people like other young people whose faith is dynamic and visible. Youth Alpha or Youth Emmaus courses are an important resource, and are better held in a school or a home than on church premises. Peer-led youth cells are increasingly important.[24] The intention will be to reconnect believing, belonging and behaving. Leslie Francis and Robin Gill have both emphasized the symbiotic relationship between the three.

There is a direct link between regular church attendance and the maintenance of historic biblical Christian belief. Precisely what sort of 'church' is needed for young people will be addressed below (and by Chris Russell in Chapters 8 and 9), but those who attend regularly tend to have a stronger commitment to historic Christian belief than those who come occasionally. The occasional attenders are more 'orthodox' than those who never attend. As church attendance involves worship and education rooted in the Christian faith, this should not be surprising. Christian worship and fellowship is a vital component of discipleship. Believing needs to be sustained by belonging, which includes the example of other Christians, and teaching. There is also evidence that regular worshippers sustain higher levels of love for others, self-worth and Christian morality! Behaving needs to be sustained by belonging and believing.

7 Youth ministry recognizes the importance of discipleship

The challenge and resources for growth in discipleship are particularly urgent in our consumer society. Consumerism tends to reduce everything to an object for my pleasure and is toxic for long-term commitment. Youth cultures used to take a subcultural form, with clear boundaries and an ethic of group loyalty. This is long gone.

> Young people appear to consume the Christian scene in roughly the same way they consume other scenes. That is, they move from one to the other fairly easily and construct their identities from whatever takes their fancy. The exclusivity that characterised both youth culture and the Christian youth culture in the last few decades has largely collapsed.[25]

Today's charismatic youth movements need to be particularly alert. A consumer society encourages a quest for a religious buzz, rather than for a life of discipleship. Rock-accompanied worship songs and charismatic experiences can be consumed for their own sake as, for that matter, can Taizé events. Consumer culture does not discriminate. Christian pastoral work with young people will need to re-establish the link between spirituality and ethics.

As Tim Sudworth describes in Chapter 1, an earlier generation of Evangelical youth ministry had a very strong protectionist agenda.[26] It often combined a theology of separation from 'the world', with the anxieties of churchgoing parents about their children's need of protection from the temptations of teenage life. Whatever the strengths and weaknesses of that approach, contemporary digitally mediated youth culture is not avoidable. It is not possible to live apart from it and have a normal life. Christian discipleship is about living within it as a follower of Christ. Both youth leaders and Christian parents have to learn to trust God to protect their young people 'in' the world, while helping them to live distinctive and potentially transformative Christian lives among their peers. A negative policy of protection equips them to fail as adult Christians. What is needed is training in discernment – teaching discernment in context, by being with them in their world and helping them to see it through Christ's eyes

> **Both youth leaders and Christian parents have to learn to trust God to protect their young people 'in' the world, while helping them to live distinctive and potentially transformative Christian lives among their peers.**

and live in it Christ's way. Teaching programmes need to be based around real-life situations. They should begin with the situation, and go from there to the Bible, at least as often as the other way round. Youth cells should be developed for mutual lifestyle support. Youth leaders and parents need to trust God in their young people (at least) as much as they trust him in themselves!

Having outlined the distinctives of youth ministry, I would like to move on to consider some particular dilemmas faced by the Church in its work with young people.

Youth congregations

I have been involved in Christian youth ministry since being brought to faith through Crusaders when I was eight. In my view today's youth ministry faces a particular dilemma. When ministry is culturally appropriate, because the incarnational principle is being followed, it is easier to win young people to Christ than it has been for many years. Simultaneously it is harder to integrate them into the existing church than I can ever remember. The days of a youth fellowship meeting in a home midweek and then all being in one of their church's main services on a Sunday are largely gone.

> When ministry is culturally appropriate, because the incarnational principle is being followed, it is easier to win young people to Christ than it has been for many years. Simultaneously it is harder to integrate them into the existing church than I can ever remember.

The phenomenon of youth congregations has come into being as a result. I have written about this in detail elsewhere[27] and Avril Baigent considers this question from a Roman Catholic perspective in Chapter 5. In my view, there is no theological justification for aiming at a single-generation church, although many churches with elderly congregations have just that. However, there is ample justification for a youth congregation as a targeted part of a parish, benefice or deanery's overall strategy and there are several examples featured in this book (e.g. Eden, in Chapter 5). In the diocese of Canterbury, where I work, one team ministry decided to employ a youth minister, rather than a priest, in order to develop a youth congregation across their town.[28]

The Archbishops' evangelistic initiative Springboard discovered that congregations with young people tended to attract the other age groups as well.[29] But to have and keep young people requires providing them with appropriate space to meet with their peers, as well as opportunities to serve their communities. The strongest argument for youth congregations is the missiological one. We need to plant the gospel into their generation, which I see as the first generation in a cultural era that could well survive for many generations.[30] At the time of writing there were 73 youth congregations registered on the Fresh Expressions web site.[31] There is a variety of models. Youth congregations can be a new congregation of an existing church.

They can be regular area celebrations (like Pulse, see Chapter 5), run in a deanery (like Eden, Chapter 5), a secondary school catchment area, or as an ecumenical exercise, supported by youth cells within the sponsoring churches. They can be church plants.[32] These are not youth events run by adults, although there will be adult supervision. A youth worker may well be in overall charge, but the young people are taking responsibility for church, its worship, ministry and mission.

Leadership

The substantial changes in practice outlined above have also required a revolution in youth leadership. Many churches now have full- or part-time youth ministers. Full-time youth ministers are now trained very differently from previous generations. The pivotal change came with the founding of the Centre for Youth Ministry in 1996.[33] A partnership of youth ministry organizations and theological colleges combined to offer a degree in Youth, Community and Applied Theology together with a professional JNC qualification. This training was the vision of Pete Ward and Bob Mayo. It combined the experience of youth work organizations which had reinvented themselves to face the realities of the 1990s with the expertise of the statutory youth service, but without the highly secular assumptions that underlie most courses accredited by the National Youth Agency. NYA accreditation would not have been achieved if the partners in CYM had applied individually. However, once the door to accreditation for faith organizations had been opened Moorlands Bible College and the Oasis Trust were also able to gain accreditation.

The impact of this has been substantial. There were soon more JNC-qualified youth workers being employed by the churches than by the statutory youth service! But more importantly, the training had raised the standard of what could reasonably be expected of youth ministry. This increase in professional standards also required churches to be more professional in their support and management of youth workers. Amaze (the Association of Christian Youth and Children's Workers) was formed to act as a strategic resource to youth workers and those seeking help in managing them.[34]

Better training for youth ministers only provides one part of the solution. There is a danger that churches employ a youth minister and then assume that they have nothing else to do. A good youth minister will train volunteer leaders and equip young people to exercise their ministries. This will create work for churches, not delegate it away. It will also require financial commitment and realistic budgets.

Conclusion: a critical time

This is a critical time for the Church's ministry among young people. The vast majority of children and young people are the 'non-churched'.[35] They know little if anything of the Christian faith and often have little sense of need for God, the transcendent or the spiritual. There has to be a long-term strategy of sowing the gospel story back into our culture. Our Church schools provide us with a huge opportunity. Many churches have no young people of secondary age. At the same time church-based youth ministry has never been more imaginative. Youth ministry that equips young people to win their friends to faith, within a bigger vision of the world-transforming power of the kingdom of God, is the most significant resource God has given us.

> **❝This is a critical time for the Church's ministry among young people. The vast majority of children and young people are the 'non-churched'. They know little if anything of the Christian faith and often have little sense of need for God, the transcendent or the spiritual. There has to be a long-term strategy of sowing the gospel story back into our culture.❞**

3 The ever-changing context of young people
Tim Sudworth

Mission-shaped Church explored, in general terms, the culture and environment in which the Church exists as the context in which it needs to do mission. After prayer, that context needs to be our starting point too when we're exploring how to connect with young people in our area. We need to consider the 'global village' in which young people operate, the government policies that affect their lives, the national Church situation, and more locally how young people are living in and engaging with the communities that we seek to serve.

We are facing a significant, and some would say a critical, challenge as the Western Church. When, in 2004, the Church of England published its attendance figures, there was a media frenzy of headlines predicting its death by 2040. (It seems ironic that even though the figures for 2004 showed that there was a slow down in the decline, and slight growth in some areas, the media still focused on 'decline'.[1]) We, and the young people we serve, are living in a culture that is continually changing and in which market and social forces are operating the like of which we have never seen before. Nor could we have expected these forces to have such power and influence over our young people.

Martin Lindstrom, in his book *Brandchild*, notes that young people have 'grown up faster, are more connected, more direct and more informed. They have more personal power, more money, influence and attention than any other generation before them.'[2]

In *Making Sense of Generation Y* Graham Cray picks up on the same theme by summarizing David Lyon: 'Three major transitions interlock and radically change the way we experience and interpret the world. They are the shifts from producer to consumer, from industrial to electronic society and from sovereign nation states to a globalized world.'[3]

> ❝Many of us as adults struggle to keep up with and connect to the sociological and cultural climate that we inhabit. We can only imagine what life must be like for the young people who are growing up in this climate, and just accept it all as the norm.❞

Many of us as adults struggle to keep up with and connect to the sociological and cultural climate that we inhabit. We can only imagine what life must be like for the young people who are growing up in this climate, and just accept it all as the norm.

Global youth

In *Brandchild* Martin Lindstrom explores the minds of today's global 'kids' and their relationships with brands. He does this as a marketing guru, who offers insights into young people's lives so companies can target them more efficiently with their products. He asserts that 'No other generation has ever had so much disposable income as this one. So it is no coincidence that this emerging generation has become powerful enough to have a specific allotment in every marketing director's budget.'[4]

Cray picks up on this 'right to consume' in *Making Sense of Generation Y*. Where once we found our identity and therefore meaning in what we produced, we now find meaning and fulfilment in what we choose. Religion has become just another consumer choice. The challenge for the Church then is this: how do we confront a society that allows the rich to choose more, and more often, and the poor to choose less, less often?

Young people operate in an environment not restricted by geography, with friends not limited to the street, town, city or even country that they live in. According to Lindstrom, close to half the world's urban young are connected to the Internet.[5] As soon as young people connect to the Internet an icon lets them know which of their friends they can talk to through 'instant messaging'. They don't have to wait

> ❝The emphasis now is not on technology itself but, as Lindstrom suggests, on content. Young people are not impressed by what the technology *is*, but by what the technology can *give them*.❞

long for an answer; a response is almost immediate. In fact the fascination with electronic media of previous generations has been lost by this new generation, who largely see the computer as a tool. The emphasis now is not on technology itself but, as Lindstrom suggests, on content. Young people are not impressed by what the technology *is*, but by what the technology can *give them*.

Social trends of young people in the UK

Every two years the Trust for the Study of Adolescence produces a report on the latest figures with regards to young people in the UK.[6]

- There are approximately 7.8 million teenagers living in the UK (2005). Of these more than 3.8 million are between the ages of 10 and 14, while over 3.9 million are between the ages of 15 and 19.

- Children and teenagers make up a quarter of the total population of the UK, a figure roughly similar to that of other European countries.

  > Children and teenagers make up a quarter of the total population of the UK

- In Western countries over the last 30 years there has been a decrease in the stability of marriage, and an increase in cohabitation and parenthood outside marriage.

- The number of families with dependent children headed by a lone parent has increased from 8% of all families in 1971 to 25% of all families in 2004.

- While the number of lone-parent families has been increasing, the divorce rate has remained relatively stable. The 1960s and 1970s saw the highest increase, but since the mid 1990s the rate has remained relatively stable.

- In 2003, there were around 1.8 million children in workless households in the UK, the largest proportion of any European country.

Statistics from other areas paint a darker picture:

> 1 in 15 young people regularly self-harm.

- Quite possibly the most disturbing statistic of them all is that 1 in 15 young people regularly self-harm. This statistic is based on the number of young people taken into accident and emergency for the treatment of wounds brought about by self-harming. In reality the number of self-harmers is likely to be much higher due to the hidden nature of the practice.[7]

- 11% of children (1 in 9) in the UK run away from home or are forced to leave, and stay away overnight, on one or more occasion before the age of 16. It is estimated that 100,000 young people run away each year in the UK.[8]

- 31,000 children ring ChildLine each year – just to talk about bullying.[9]

> The second most common cause of death among 15- to 24-year-olds is suicide.

- The second most common cause of death among 15- to 24-year-olds is suicide. The most common cause is accidental death.[10]

- In 2004, 10,500 young people were permanently excluded from schools.[11]

This is the society in which young people are growing up and in which we serve them. It is a cultural setting of massive opportunities but at the same time one obsessed with image and the possession of the next fashion item, which will be out of date or broken before long.

We live in a fragmented society with young people and children manifesting many symptoms of that brokenness. In many ways our society has changed massively since the Children Act of 1989 when the 'well-being of the child' was at the forefront. We have seen a move away from the vision of the Children Act to the Every Child Matters agenda, which now sees the child as an economic commodity that could and should contribute to the well-being of society, instead of seeing young people and children as individuals in need of love and care, from inside the safety of a family and a wider caring community.

Questions for discussion

1. What do you know about the young people who live in your area? What are the schools like that they go to? Where do they hang out? What facilities are there for them? Which of the trends outlined above have the greatest impact on them?

2. How can you find out what their needs are – physical, emotional, educational and spiritual? What other agencies can you work with to discover more about the real needs of the young people in your area?

3. Which of these needs does your church or youth ministry already meet? How do you need to develop to better serve the young people in your area? Do you feel drawn to work with a particular group?

4. How often do you specifically pray for the needs and situations of young people?

5. Do we really want young people as part of our church? Our initial response is probably to say 'Of course!' But what does our practice – the way we treat young people in our churches – say?

Part Two

What's happening?
Case studies of emerging/fresh expressions

We've explored the history and mission-shaped values of youth ministry and taken a brief look at the context in which young people live. Maybe you've been left with more questions than answers; perhaps you're terrified of what lies ahead.

Some wisdom from a Peanuts cartoon may help. To set the scene: Lucy is running a psychologist's booth and Charlie Brown stops for some advice:

> *Lucy:* Life is like a deckchair, Charlie. On the cruise ship of life, some people place their deckchair at the rear of the ship, so they can see where they have been. Others place their deckchair at the front of the ship, so they can see where they are going. Which way is your deckchair facing?
>
> *Charlie:* Heck, I can't even get my deckchair unfolded.

Perhaps you are feeling a bit like Charlie Brown, tangled up in a contraption that other people seem able to master but which to you looks like a tangled mess. Hopefully, the case studies here will help you think through which way you are going – or at least they might help you to put the deckchair up.

The case studies that follow come from a diverse spectrum of churchmanship, from the charismatic through evangelical to catholic and Catholic churches, and from the middle-class suburban to working-class, north and south. For ease of reading, the projects have been sorted into four different categories:

- schools-based projects

- congregation-based projects

- young people outside the Church

- creative approaches to prayer and sacraments.

Try not to limit your reading to your own comfort zone, place or experience. All of these projects offer particular challenges to the way we do things, so read them all and hear what they have to say to you.

4 Schools-based projects

Many youth ministers go into schools on a formal or informal basis as part of their work. Some people are even employed to work full-time in schools. Many volunteers and paid workers spend a lot of time supporting and encouraging work in schools, and it's important to evaluate what is being done and to learn from it. I hope that these two case studies will enable you to reflect on the work that you already do and will give you a new challenge or vision as to where your work could go next.

The Grow project, Oxford Diocese
Mark Berry

History and background

The purpose of this case study is not to provide a model or to dig too deeply into the lives of the young people I have worked with. I could fill a book with their stories, but they are theirs to share not mine. My aim is to give you a potted history of our project, its vision and practice.

The Grow project evolved from four starting places. First, the Deanery of Mursley had been a leader in youth work in the Diocese of Oxford for many years, running very well-attended summer camps and monthly deanery youth events. Secondly, Revd John Russell, the area dean who was a half-time parish priest and half-time deanery youth chaplain, saw the need to rethink the youth work in the deanery. Numbers had been falling at events and he recognized that the changing culture required new ideas and practice. Thirdly, a family in the deanery responded to the need for more resources to go into youth work and pledged themselves to fund a worker for three years. Then fourthly, I met with John in the summer of 2001 to discuss a youth ministry for young people both in and outside of the churches.

At the first meeting we began to explore a vision which would take two years and many mistakes to pin down! For many people, the vision itself has been a stumbling block, as it does not explicitly refer to an increase in church attendance or membership as a method or an outcome of the project. It became clear as the vision developed that, for the best of reasons, many see mission as equated with church or youth group growth.

What does mission mean in Grow project?

The purpose of mission, as the project sees it, is to enable young people to experience the grace of God and to live life the way God intended in all its fullness, in relationship with and in worship of God. This means enabling young people to understand their place as part of a global Church and a wider community, but also to see how they might relate to a traditional church structure, which for many has itself become a stumbling block to the gospel. The vision speaks of a need to plant the gospel into the very heart of the culture and community of young people. In our context, this heart was identified as the school.

The vision of the project reflects a belief that church as an institution is not accessible to many of the people in our community who have no grounding in religious or Christian culture. Yet it is still the Church's commission to take the gospel to all people. Therefore, we believe that we need to encourage people to grow church in their own culture, with a language and symbols that reflect their own spiritual stories.

Bishop Mike Hill, who was Area Bishop of Buckingham until 2003 and is now Bishop of Bristol, said that church planting is too often understood as planting a culture and structure that models those existing in the mother church. Instead, we should look to plant the gospel and nurture what grows. Or as *Mission-shaped Church* states, 'The change is to an outward focus; from a "come to us" approach to a "we will go to you" attitude, embodying the gospel where people are, rather than embodying it where we are, and in ways we prefer.'[1] We share in the belief that deaneries have a strategic significance in new mission: 'Deaneries have the potential to bring together a range of human and financial resources, to consider mission beyond parish boundaries, and to share prayer and encouragement.'[2] Therefore Grow project is both a part of the deanery and commissioned by the deanery in its name to support, equip and care for all young people in its area, both spiritually and pastorally.

What about our existing young people?

I have been asked on numerous occasions, 'Why this focus on mission? What about the nurture of our existing young people?' My response has been to ask the question: 'What young people?' Is this lack of young people the result of the failure of youth work? While I am happy to take some responsibility, there are a number of factors that need to be recognized.

First, young people's time and activities are much more organized today. Many sporting activities take place on Sunday mornings, the time of traditional church services. It is hard for youth work and church to compete with other leisure activities or with homework. Secondly, it needs to be recognized that most thriving youth groups of the past had a membership that consisted mainly of children of church families. The challenge we face is not simply young people leaving church for 'better' activities, but that we are simply not engaging with non-churched teenagers (those who have never been to church), de-churched teenagers (those who used to come but have now stopped) or young families, a fact which is well illustrated by the age demographic of our congregations.

> ❝The challenge we face is not simply young people leaving church for 'better' activities, but that we are simply not engaging with non-churched teenagers (those who have never been to church), de-churched teenagers (those who used to come but have now stopped) or young families.❞

The development of the project

In a rural deanery it is almost impossible to spread one person across the whole area. The Buckingham education system is a selective one that retains the 11+ examination, which means that the few young people who do come to church are far more likely to attend private schools, faith schools or grammar schools than in the national demographic. We decided to root the project in the Cottesloe School, a secondary modern school, whose catchment area largely reflects the boundaries of the deanery. So inevitably the project was likely to engage with non-church-attending young people. As the project has a missionary focus we did not see this as a problem. However, it has to be acknowledged that many people in the churches did! Further, if the vision demands the planting of the gospel into community then it is not appropriate to visit numerous schools. We need to live and minister within one community and one school.

Developing relationships with senior staff

It was essential to develop a real working relationship with the senior staff of the school. I began by arranging a meeting with the head and asked her how I could help her and her team to develop the school, its pastoral care and environment. She was very keen to be involved in the project and has always seen it as adding value to the school. I think that a large part of this has to do with our attitude. We felt it important to begin by being honest, by explaining what the project was about and stressing that we saw mission as much more than simply evangelism. We also wanted to support the young people pastorally and spiritually.

This approach differed from other strategies of schools work. We did not want to run a Christian Union and serve only those young people who feel able to define themselves as Christian. Nor did we want to get involved with ostensibly secular activities, such as football or drama, and then seek opportunities for proclamation. Nor did we want to simply offer pastoral support. We began to talk to the school about ministry and mission, seeing my role as a priest rather than a chaplain – that is, someone who is there as an advocate, counsellor, a spiritual guide and a part of daily school life rather than as a figure of authority who is there when needed to give pastoral support or to teach.

Developing relationships with the young people

Being able to build relationships with the young people in the school was obviously vital and fortunately we have been able to connect with them very successfully. Again it was important to be honest and open about our faith and the reason we were in school. While I have been involved in all sorts of projects and activities within the life of the school, my faith and the vision of the project have always been made clear. No one has questioned whether we have some hidden agenda, because it has always been out in the open. Because of our relationship with staff I have been free to walk around the school and speak with anyone.

This has led to most, if not all, of the young people being aware of me and feeling able to simply come up and talk. Aside from the young people attending activities that we run, I have had many significant conversations in and around the playground, which have led to relationships and counselling opportunities developing.

> Because of our relationship with staff I have been free to walk around the school and speak with anyone. This has led to most, if not all, of the young people being aware of me and feeling able to simply come up and talk.

The ministry in the school

121

121 is a regular time slot on Thursday lunchtimes available for private conversations. It has been a hugely fruitful experience. Many young people come to talk about their lives and some have begun to see it as a regular part of their week. The time has been spent either in the library or walking around the school. There hasn't been a single 121 where a significant conversation with a young person has not taken place. The school suffers from a lack of external pastoral resources, as most do, and we have been able to fill some of the gaps.

However, this is not the only reason for doing 121 – pastoral concern is not divorced from spirituality and many of the conversations have moved through both areas, led by the young people themselves. Relationships built in 121 times have led to several young people beginning to come to the SPIRITzone and to SPIRITzoneLATE.

SPIRITzone and SPIRITzoneLATE

The SPIRITzone has been, for me, the most exciting part of the ministry, with young people coming each week to have conversations about life and spirituality. Numbers have varied between 6 and 80 with a core of about 20 young people. The nature of the group changes as the membership evolves and as the young people move through the school. Some groups have been really keen to be challenged and to explore relevant issues widely, some have been more difficult to keep focused. For many young people this has been the only opportunity they have had to talk about spirituality, and they have been very keen to discuss all sorts of topics and areas, including the meaning of dreams, life after death, forgiveness, fear, hope, family, religion, love, charity and, of course, God. Not all young people are concerned with spirituality, but many are and most of these do not even begin to think that church is a place to explore it. Many have expressed a concern that the Church is hypocritical and unconcerned with them. In fact one young man said, 'The church has denied me the right to seek God!'

The aim of SPIRITzone is not to teach or to Christianize the young people but to be a safe place to share stories and to explore spirituality. The group is both inclusive and egalitarian. Everyone has a right to tell his or her story and to be listened to and respected by the others there, including the leaders. SPIRITzone has in some ways become 'church'. It has a sense of community, with young people coming from most year groups, a definite purpose to seek and explore spirituality, and the attendees show a genuine respect for each other. However it would be difficult, due to the timescale, for it to actually be 'church'. Stuart Murray Williams says that while we used to talk about a period of around five to seven years for someone to come to faith, we now have to expect that it may take ten years from the initial contact, through to a point of

> ❝SPIRITzone has in some ways become 'church'. It has a sense of community, with young people coming from most year groups, a definite purpose to seek and explore spirituality, and the attendees show a genuine respect for each other. ❞

acceptance of Jesus as saviour.[3] This is a long time, especially in the lives of young people, and means that we need to stay with young people right the way through their secondary education and beyond. We have not been able to do this yet, although we have seen a number of young people take serious steps toward God and some have continued to pursue their quest after leaving the school.

The content of SPIRITzone has changed over the years depending on the people who come. We have simply sat and had a group conversation, or watched videos and discussed their theme. Young people have brought things in to talk about. We often cover the floor with cards and provide pens and paint to respond creatively to a question or idea. On other occasions, we have split into small groups and used mind-maps to explore a question. It does take time each year to re-establish the sense of belonging and find a new way to talk as new young people come and older ones leave.

We have recently started to create a space for deeper thought and reflection which we call SPIRITzoneLATE. It is attended by young people from both church and SPIRITzone. The evening normally takes the form of positioning prayer stations, Scripture texts, poems, images and activities around the drama studio, with a café space to provide a chance to talk and share thoughts from the stations. The attendance has been small, but the time and experience valuable.

Peer support, peer education and the school council

During our time in the school we have been instrumental in developing peer support and peer education programmes with both the school and statutory services. The peer support programme trains around 70 young people from Years 10 and 11 in listening and basic pastoral skills and then assigns them to a Year 7 or 8 form group. The aim is to provide a safe way for the younger school members to talk about any problems or concerns that they might have. A number of the peer supporters also run a lunchtime youth club for Year 7s to increase the contact, to give them a safe place to chat and to provide a link to members of staff and to me.

The peer education programme trains sixth-form students to lead group sessions with Year 7s on issues such as puberty and identity. At the request of the school we have set up a school council structure which allows the young people to get involved in the management and running of the school.

In addition, two years ago I was asked to be a school governor with an oversight of the spiritual development of the school and a responsibility to ensure that the student voice is heard. I am not naturally a committee person, but this has been a real opportunity to help shape the ethos of the school.

What do these pastoral projects have to do with mission? First, pastoral care is a duty of all ministries. Secondly, mission entails more than evangelism. It also includes pastoral care, social justice and liberation – the kingdom of heaven on earth, where young people feel able to change their environment for the better and know that their voices are heard. Thirdly, words without deeds are meaningless. It is important that love is practical and is seen in action, otherwise it is simply a 'clanging cymbal' (1 Corinthians 13.1).

Conclusion: lessons learnt

The bottom line for all of us involved in Grow project had been 'sharing life' (1 Thessalonians 2.8) and so much of my time has been spent simply being with people in the community, listening to them, learning from them and sharing my God story. The most important aspect of Grow project for me has been the hundreds of relationships that we have been able to develop, each one founded on a desire to help others to define their 'unknown god' stories (Acts 17.23). It is integral to our vision that we have no hidden agenda, that we are open and honest. The foundation of our project is a belief that most people are interested in spirituality even though a growing number have never heard the gospel. I have found no resistance from either young people or staff to talk about their beliefs and to share their stories. In fact, the opposite is true. Many young people and staff over the last three and a half years have communicated their surprise that the Church is actually interested in them. People want to be listened to, they want the chance to ask questions and to explore, and they want to hear what we have to say. But it seems that the majority are not going to come to church to find out more!

> ❝Many young people and staff over the last three and a half years have communicated their surprise that the Church is actually interested in them. People want to be listened to, they want the chance to ask questions and to explore, and they want to hear what we have to say.❞

Youth ministry based in high schools, Blackburn Diocese

Peter Ballard

The philosopher Arthur Schopenhauer once said, 'Our task is not to see the things other people do not see but to think things other people do not think about that which everybody sees.'[4]

History and background

When the Blackburn Diocesan Board of Education first considered the idea of focusing its youth work in high schools, it could have been interpreted as just another fad – the latest idea in response to the constant call in the Church to find new ways of being church. However, the seeds of this development had been sown, albeit unknowingly, many years before.

A chance meeting in 1991 opened a door which over the years has led to a great deal of exciting work with young people. The churches of Lancaster had organized a big 'It's a Knock Out' competition which aimed to draw together churches in the area and raise funds for the Church Urban Fund. The parish of which I was then vicar had entered a team and we made it into the final. The team we needed to beat was captained by Brian McConkey, an ebullient youth worker from the large evangelical parish in the city. He was as passionate to win as we were. I don't remember the exact words of the tirade I received during the last game, but suffice it to say it was not complimentary. It was not helped by the history of the two parishes, which had in the past been seen as being at opposite ends of the spectrum. However, the passion with which it was delivered led to a professional relationship and a friendship which was not only to break down many barriers of churchmanship but which also made me realize that whatever we did in our work with young people, we had to be totally committed, prepared to think the unthinkable and do the things which others would claim to be impossible. It is vital that all our work in the Church comes from a vocation about which we are passionate. That chance meeting was to have much to answer for in the future.

A few years later, Brian and I came to work closely together and he took me on a journey that opened my eyes. He provided the opportunity for me to meet young people in all sorts of different situations. It has been one of the greatest privileges of my ministry to be allowed to share some of their journey through life. It was Brian who dragged me through the gardens of Lambeth Palace during 'Time of our Lives' to hear the confession of a young adult who had been so moved by some of the events that weekend that she wanted to pour her heart out to somebody.[5] I am not sure she understood about sacramental confession but Brian got alongside her as only he could do. A week later she wrote to thank us both for opening the doors for her to continue her journey with Christ.

> ❛We realized that we were looking for young people in churches to share and to work with when actually there were hundreds of such young people, not in our parishes, but in our high schools.❜

In those years we went on many 'McConkey's Tours', which gave me quality time to be with young people and young adults and to listen and share with them. We did a number of youth missions in different parishes, where we would develop and lead Sunday worship with a team of young people. These went well, but some times we became a little despondent at the lack of young people over the age of 13. We realized that we were looking for young people in churches to share and to work with when actually there were hundreds of such young people, not in our parishes, but in our high schools. What could we achieve if we could get alongside young people in the schools?

Developing the vision

Like most dioceses, Blackburn had one youth officer who was ably supported by a large number of willing volunteers. If we were going to get alongside these young people, we had to work with them where they were not just for a few hours or even for a week a year, but all the time. The idea that we might have a team of youth officers, employed by the diocese but each based in a school, was thinking the unthinkable. I can still hear the vicar of a large parish telling me that if I thought for one minute that parishes were paying their parish share to fund lots of youth officers, I could forget it.

Archbishop Oscar Romero wrote, 'We plant the seeds that one day will grow. We water the seeds already planted knowing they hold future promise.

We lay foundations that will need further development.'[6] The seed had been planted. No matter how often it was dismissed as being fanciful and undeliverable, we could not deny that high schools were the place where young people were to be found, not the pews of our parishes. It was also undeniable that the young people who were in our parishes were also in our high schools. There were many reasons why it might not work, not least money, but if we were to develop the idea further we needed the support of our high schools. The biggest fear was not that the high school wouldn't want a youth worker, but they would want one so much we would end up disappointing them if we couldn't deliver.

The question now was what did we want to deliver and how could we achieve it? If we have lost touch with young people, it follows we have lost touch with their families. As the seed began to grow we were no longer merely looking at our high schools as places where we could meet young people, we were now looking at new forms of church and new forms of parish. The vision that was unfolding was of a youth worker/chaplain working in the school alongside young people, but also in the places where they lived and played. If somebody in the school had a relative who was ill, it was the youth worker/chaplain we saw visiting, not a local clergyman who had no other contact with the family. Schools are vibrant communities, and we wanted our youth worker/chaplains to also work with the staff and the extended community which surrounds any school. By the time we were talking to heads and governors, we had developed a vision of a school as a parish church and all those involved with it as the parish. We were turning upside down and inside out the model of minister and parish which had existed in the Diocese of Blackburn for the whole of its 75-year history.

> If we have lost touch with young people, it follows we have lost touch with their families. As the seed began to grow we were no longer merely looking at our high schools as places where we could meet young people, we were now looking at new forms of church and new forms of parish.

Opposition to the vision

Persuading heads and governors that they might like to be a part of this new venture was easy. The hardest people to convince were those that you would have expected to be the driving force behind the decision. The diocesan youth committee and others who had devoted a lot of time to developing youth work in the diocese questioned whether this was really youth work at all. Our faith is in the death and resurrection of Jesus. But for some allowing what we had to die so that a new venture could rise up was too great a risk and a step too far. For some the dream was too radical and, despite our best efforts, they resigned. For others it was an opportunity to move on and for many it was never going to be reality unless we could solve the fundamental problem of funding. It was also vital to make sure that we got across the message that putting 'bums on seats' was not a criterion of the success of this project.

Who is going to pay for it? Funding the vision

For some years the Board of Education had been repositioning itself and had developed into a major provider of education resources both in the diocese and beyond. As a consequence it was in a healthy financial position and was able to make some funds available for a new venture. Other money came through the Church Commissioners, who had given their extra funds to dioceses for mission, with the encouragement to be creative in their use. Together we created a pot of £750,000 to be used over a five-year period to turn the vision into reality.

Who will do the work? Finding the right people

By now we had three schools interested in having a youth worker/chaplain and the funding to turn dreams into reality. We were still being heavily criticized by those who saw this as a move away from traditional youth work, but the time had come to test the market.

From the outset, it had been important to establish that while this was a joint position, in that the youth worker would need to work closely with the heads, schools, parishes and diocese, the actual appointment was a diocesan one. At the end of the day the diocese would have the right of veto. We were determined that we would only appoint people whom we believed to be of the right calibre and it would be better for the project not to get off the ground than for it to be undermined because we had appointed the wrong people. If we got this right, we would have a new ministry in our schools, but we would also have a group of people who could provide support across the diocese to parishes and individuals. We imagined a diverse team with complementary gifts and

> ❝We wanted to appoint the best people for the job, but we also had a longing that at least one of them would be ordained so we wouldn't end up with people drawing the conclusion that the dog collar is a bar to working with young people.❞

talents. We wanted to appoint the best people for the job, but we also had a longing that at least one of them would be ordained so we wouldn't end up with people drawing the conclusion that the dog collar is a bar to working with young people. It was vital to us that this team should give people a model which was transferable into local parishes and beyond.

Had we known at the beginning how difficult it could be to find suitable people, we might have given up before even advertising the posts. To make sure we kept the youth lobby happy we advertised in several youth worker magazines and several other publications as well as the *Church Times* and locally. The lack of an overwhelming positive response shocked us. We accepted that we were dealing with a new concept. But it had been decided to remunerate this position at the same rate as an incumbent, so in youth-work terms we were offering an awful lot of money and either housing or a housing allowance.

Realizing the vision

It took 18 months from the first discussions to Susie Mapledoram walking through the doors of St Michael's Church of England High School in Chorley as our first youth worker/chaplain. From that moment, lights flashed and bells rang and it was clear that the seed that we had watered had burst into bloom. Our first round of adverts had brought us two people but further attempts at advertising did not meet with much success and so we ended up headhunting for our third post.

The role of the youth worker/chaplain within the school

The role of the youth worker/chaplain varies from school to school but basically the first call on time is to be a listening ear and to 'loiter with intent'. In the first year the challenges were wide and varied. It has been vital to provide the young people with a 'listening ear' which is somewhat detached from the formal structure of the school. At the same time it has been important to be a bridge between all the different areas of school and community life. A major task has been the development of collective worship and opportunities for people to discuss and grow in their faith. The social or pastoral nature of the work has ranged from helping people come to terms with illness to helping with bereavement. The presence of a youth worker/chaplain within the formal structure of the schools has opened to the door to legitimizing time in the curriculum for spirituality and moral development, giving young people, some for the first time, the opportunity to develop and grow spiritually. This has all had a noticeable link back to parish life, making vital links between what happens on a Sunday and during the rest of the week.

Conclusion

Other schools are now interested and the dream is to have ten such posts across the diocese. The success of the first appointments is clear for all to see. It has, at times, been a struggle to get the parishes local to the schools to see the youth worker/chaplain as a facilitator and trainer in their parishes and not just someone there 'to do the youth work' for them. They are there to help sow seeds and to challenge all of us to think outside the box as we follow in the footsteps of Jesus.

Questions for discussion

1. How important are schools in the developing mission of our local churches? If that's where young people are, in what ways can we take church to them instead of expecting them to come to us?

2. What constraints might there be on Christians who work in the context of formal education? Conversely, what unique opportunities are there?

3. What natural links does your church already have with local schools – as pupils, parents, governors, teachers, non-teaching staff? How can you build on these links?

4. What opportunities are there to develop this kind of work in your local schools? What steps do you need to take to start?

5. GROW project was a deanery initiative; the second case study was a diocesan intiative. Are there opportunities for your church to work with others in your area, deanery or diocese to resource work with young people in schools?

6. Think about the diverse range of young people found at your local school. Do we really want all these young people as part of our church? What might we need to change so that they feel welcome?

Further resources

For more on schools work, see:

David Lankshear, *Churches Serving Schools*, Church House Publishing, 2002.

Debbie Orriss, 'Class Act: developing schools work', in David Booker (ed.), *Young People and Mission*, Church House Publishing, 2007.

Margaret Withers, *Mission-shaped Children*, Church House Publishing, 2006. See especially ch. 8: 'School: an all-age Christian community'.

5 Congregation-based projects

As you will see from this section youth services and congregations come in very different forms and structures but the focus is the same – giving young people a safe space in which to engage in an appropriate form of worship. A *youth service* may be defined as an occasional worship event designed for and sometimes by young people. A *youth congregation* is usually more fixed and regular, and may meet on a weekly basis alongside other congregations of a church.[1]

In Chapter 2, Graham Cray touched upon some of the issues around youth congregations which are entirely separate from the rest of the church and at the end of this section, Avril Baigent, a youth worker in the Roman Catholic Diocese of Northampton, asks some important questions about how the Body of Christ can function as God intended if it is split along generational lines.

Pulse, Chorleywood

Mark Russell

Pulse is a monthly youth worship event run by a number of churches in the Chorleywood area, a largely middle-class area just outside the M25 in Hertfordshire.

The vision for Pulse

Pulse started as a result of a brainstorm with the local youth workers in the Chorleywood area. The vision was to create a worship evening which would reach out to young people in our area with the good news of Jesus. We wanted Pulse to be an event that would be well-run, professional, relevant, punchy and different, an event which would dare to take risks for the gospel and be creative in style. Our aims for Pulse were:

1. to excite and release young people to use their gifts in ministry and worship;

2. to enthuse young people to serve in their individual churches;

3. to provide a resource that would give Christian young people confidence to invite their non-Christian mates along, and for them to be challenged with the gospel;

4. to build unity among young people from different churches;

5. to be a catalyst for social action in the local community.

The format

Pulse takes place on the last Friday evening of each month. The planning team, made up of adult volunteers and young people, decided to use Christ Church, which is a Victorian Anglican church complete with chancel and stone pulpit. It's a beautiful building, but one that needs a little work to make it look cool! So each month a team of young people transform the church building. They move the chairs, put up sound and light rigging, and hang black drapes and banners over the walls. The result is a culturally relevant-looking, spacious and comfortable worship space that feels welcoming and non-threatening to young people. Using an old building in a new way on a different day of the week to normal is exciting. The worship service at Pulse uses multi-media, contemporary worship. It has a focus on intercessory prayer, and a commitment to relevant Bible teaching. We try to use a different running order each month. Sometimes we have group work and discussion; sometimes we use silence; sometimes we have food!

At Pulse, young people lead the worship, play in the band and preach from time to time. They work the lighting and the sound, they set up and they tear down each event. The young people run Pulse, and therefore have total confidence to invite their mates along to it. We started with around 50 young people per month, and now we have anywhere from 150 to 250 per month, which is awesome. The core attendees are churched young people but increasingly more unchurched young people are coming along.

The challenges

Of course Pulse has its challenges. Young people are full of enthusiasm and zeal, and occasionally as leaders we have to channel that enthusiasm in an appropriate direction! Running a large event together with lots of churches both large and small has its tensions. But there is a real sense of trust between all the leaders. We believe that the event's vision is good and is blessed by God. We need to see our work as kingdom work, rather than merely aiming to bless or grow an individual parish church. There is a risk that as different youth groups come together for worship, some young people may well decide they would rather be a part of another group. As a team we have had to face this inter-group migration, which causes its own challenges to the youth leaders. There is a further risk in that we have a large number of young people coming and they could cause damage to the church premises – and sometimes do. We have had the odd doughnut walked into the carpet and the occasional glass of coke spilled. We have had to put people in place to keep a watchful eye, but our philosophy is that the church building was built to be used. All of us agree that despite the challenges and the risks, the blessings and benefits of this event are very significant indeed.

Key achievements of Pulse

- Pulse has brought together young people from a number of churches, not least a number of small churches, whose young people really benefit from being in the larger group.

- Pulse has built a fresh unity and trust among the youth leaders from the local churches that are involved.

- Young people are involved in planning, leading and promoting Pulse at every level. Pulse has been a real school of ministry training, and is raising up a new generation of young leaders. Pulse takes young people's contributions seriously.

- The growth of Pulse has brought fresh inspiration and growth to each of the churches involved in the project. Their young people have been envisioned and empowered at Pulse, and so can use those skills and gifts in the local church setting as well.

- Pulse has seen an explosion of new people come along, invited by their mates in school, and so has been a safe place for young people to explore what the Christian faith is all about. As one young guy who had never been to church before put it to me, 'Pulse doesn't feel like Church!'

- Pulse has taken seriously its passion to help the young people put their faith into social action. We have had a number of community days, built on the principles of the Noise Project from Soul Survivor. We have encouraged our young people to do prayer walks in the area, and also serve practically in the local community. We are passionate about helping our young people see the importance of living out their faith in their school and in the local setting.

- Pulse depends on resources from the local churches involved, and also the commitment and vision of a number of people who give their time, talents and equipment freely. In particular, Paul Davison, our sound engineer, has been at almost every Pulse since we started, and brings all the sound equipment with him.

What next?

One of the great challenges of being church in the twenty-first century is to present the unchanging truth of the gospel of Christ in a new way to a fast-changing world. We need to do church in new ways, and to design a model that fits the needs of the particular mission context. Pulse is a prime example of doing a new thing, taking risks and seeking to build unity in the mission of the Church.

> We need to do church in new ways, and to design a model that fits the needs of the particular mission context. Pulse is a prime example of doing a new thing, taking risks and seeking to build unity in the mission of the Church.

Is Pulse church?

Pulse is not in itself a church. Pulse is an event, a resource to grow a number of churches, and as that it works perfectly. Our challenge now we have built the worship service to be effective and relevant, is to do more youth work, as Pulse, in the local community. We would like to run more events like sports days, barbecues, concerts and clubs, to reach out to the young people of the wider community who do not come to Pulse. This kind of detached youth work would be really hard for an individual parish church, but because Pulse is a united venture, we can do it together. The next step for us is to inspire and envision our young people to reach out to the community in new ways. After that, I have no idea what will happen but, as a leadership team, that excites us! We keep praying and trusting God to reveal his will, and pray that he would use Pulse to change young lives with the good news of Jesus Christ.

Afterword: Dr Rowan Williams visits Pulse

In 2005 Pulse was delighted to welcome the Archbishop of Canterbury Dr Rowan Williams. During his visit, he challenged the young people to realize that church was what happened when people come together in community to encounter the presence of Jesus Christ. He challenged them to realize the spiritual wisdom in each other, and to never be afraid to talk about Jesus and ask questions. Pulse seeks to provide that vehicle for young people to encounter Jesus, to walk in community with others on that pilgrim path, and to give people a safe place to ask questions about spiritual things. Our prayer for tomorrow is that God would do even more, and expand our vision even wider, to see his purposes for our local community.

> **❝Pulse seeks to provide that vehicle for young people to encounter Jesus, to walk in community with others on that pilgrim path, and to give people a safe place to ask questions about spiritual things.❞**

Eden, Steyning, Chichester
Derek Spencer

The history and background: in the beginning

Derek Spencer moved to Steyning, West Sussex in September 2001 as the deanery youth missioner, with the aim of kick-starting youth work in the deanery and exploring the possibility of setting up a youth congregation. As very little youth work was already happening, his strategy was to start by building relationships with young people both inside and outside the church. Working with a local team, he began two deanery youth groups that ran on alternate weekends to cater for the spiritual and social needs of the young people who attended, with a joint meeting every so often. He also started to work regularly in two local schools. At Steyning Grammar School he took assemblies and lessons and did detached youth work in the boarding house of the school. And at Rydon Community College, a middle school, he worked for half a day a week, teaching RE, setting up a lunchtime Christian group and running an after-school football club. This enabled him to get to know young people who would later move up to the grammar school. After 18 months, the time seemed right to develop the work further, as Derek explains below.

Derek Spencer reports

Ever since taking on this post, my aim has been to provide some sort of relevant, credible youth setting where young people could come together and worship. I know that this was the Bishop's hope, although he never pressurized me by actually telling me that this was what he wanted to see happen. Deep down though, I knew a deanery youth congregation was high on his agenda. The problem I felt we had was that there was such a small amount of youth work happening in the area, any prospect of a youth congregation seemed a million miles away.

However, the first 18 months had gone really well. The deanery had been supportive and cooperative in providing the finances that enabled me to carry out my work. The deanery youth groups had grown and so too had my contacts with local young people. This had been partly due to my work within the local schools, but nevertheless, I felt we had achieved an awful lot in a reasonably short space of time.

The time came to move the work forward. I had been given the go-ahead to use the drama hall[2] at Steyning Grammar School as a venue for any services I wanted to hold there. I had a reasonable understanding of the people in the area, and had noticed those who I thought had a heart, a desire and an idea of what could be achieved. Along with my wife I approached six adults whom I had got to know during my time in the deanery, all from different churches, to see if they would join a team which would oversee a youth congregation. We met together, prayed and came to the conclusion that this was exactly what the deanery needed, what the young people wanted, and something we all felt extremely excited about being involved with. We came up with the name Eden, as it represented something new, a beginning, something organic. I contacted some friends who were artists to design me a logo, a template for flyers and a web site. Everything seemed to be in place: we now had a committed group of people who were prepared to meet regularly to plan, pray for and lead the services. We pencilled in 1 June 2003 for a pilot service. Eden had been conceived!

What is Eden?

This is how we describe Eden on our web site, www.edenzone.com:

> Eden is . . .
>
> . . . a monthly youth service held in Steyning Grammar School in West Sussex. It is a Church of England initiative which has been set up in the Storrington Deanery within Chichester Diocese.
>
> Eden is . . . Christian; Imaginative; Alternative; Multi-media; Relaxed; Participatory; Fresh . . .
>
> Services incorporate . . . Worship; exploring God's Word; various forms of prayer; space to respond to God. We seek to worship God in ways that young people can relate to and encourage all to participate at whatever level they feel comfortable with, recognising that we are all on a journey of faith. The aim is to be real with God.
>
> Space before and after the 'service' is equally important for relationship-building, chilling-out, and fun etc.
>
> This service is for young people, but there are no age restrictions, so whatever your age you are welcome to come and explore Eden.[3]

The launch

Having created an identity in the form of a name, we thought that for the first service we would look at the Garden of Eden and create a service around that. The title was 'Exploring Eden' and we looked at a number of themes arising from the story in Genesis – creation, relationships, identity, temptation, choices, security and the father heart of God. We would then explore these themes in more depth in subsequent services during the following year. The initial service included video loops, ambient music and different stations placed around the drama hall for people to go and explore. We had a meditation, drama and worship, as well as six 5-minute talks introducing the themes. The leadership team were all given different responsibilities to oversee certain aspects of the service. It's very difficult to do the service any justice whatsoever in writing about it – it really did need to be experienced to get a true understanding of what it was about. There were around 130 people there, 75 per cent of whom were teenagers. All I can say is that the feedback was really positive. The following day I had phone calls from many people, both young and old, saying how much they had enjoyed the whole experience and, in particular, describing their pleasure in seeing so many young people coming together to worship God. Eden had taken off.

Eden's aims

The aims of Eden are quite simple – we want to provide an interactive, relevant, credible environment for young people to come along and worship God. That doesn't mean we are encouraging young people to leave their existing church or denomination, but rather facing the fact that many young people want something more than what the local 'regular' churches can provide or are providing.

In December 2003, I was ordained and am serving out my curacy in

> The aims of Eden are quite simple – we want to provide an interactive, relevant, credible environment for young people to come along and worship God. That doesn't mean we are encouraging young people to leave their existing church or denomination, but rather facing the fact that many young people want something more than what the local 'regular' churches can provide or are providing.

this same role as deanery youth missioner. My priesting took place during an Eden service in January 2005, with the Bishop coming to the young people instead of expecting them to visit his territory. The service was a fantastic combination of two cultures within the church – the old and the new. My personal aim for Eden is that, now I have been ordained with the intention of overseeing Eden and continuing in this post, people will take seriously what we have started here. The fact that the Bishop has decided to ordain me in this post shows that he values it and I hope that this encourages others to value it too. I believe we have given birth to something which is affecting many people in a positive way. It is still early days, and the whole initiative feels rather vulnerable, so therefore it needs nurturing and establishing, so that it can continue to grow and evolve.

Life, Ashtead, Surrey
Adam Prior

The history and background

We like to think we have something pretty special at Life. I had been at St George's in Ashtead (a small suburban town on the outskirts of London) for nearly eight years. We had a really good system of youth house groups where each young person was discipled by an older Christian. We did the usual round of trips each year – Soul Survivor, parish weekend away and youth weekend away. But one thing seemed stuck, there was a real lack of engagement in the worship and community of the wider church in the evening, and by and large a lack of 'real growth' and engagement with young people outside their normal networks.

Unlike many parishes we had a lot of young people inside and outside the evening service. The ones outside tended to skate and sometimes make too much noise. The ones on the inside half-heartedly engaged with the worship, and tended not to engage with the talks at all. We were left with several questions:

- What were the young people there for?
- Should we make them behave and engage in the service better?
- Should we give them something to do to help them engage?

- What was preventing them growing in their worship in that service?

We soon realized something had to be done. We could not leave the situation as it was. But at the same time we did not want to separate off the young people from the rest of the church.

Developing the vision for Life

Over a period of a year we reviewed our youth ministry provision, read anything there was to read on the subject of youth congregations, both for and against, visited other youth congregations, prayed and waited to see what happened.

We finally decided that a youth congregation was the way forward and that the model that predominates in our churches, both locally and nationally, already supports the development of 'other' congregations. Most churches we looked at had at least two different congregations already operating. Some were based on the time of meeting (so, for example, people who cannot get to church on a Sunday come on a Wednesday), and others were based on style and content. At the same time as developing the congregation we wanted to strengthen our mission to young people and our youth home groups, as so not to lose the core of what we did. I stressed to the young people that attendance at youth house groups was more important than attendance at the youth congregation, as discipleship still had to be the most important thing that happened in our ministry.

Two years down the line we have a weekly congregation that is run totally by the young people, with upwards of 40 young people involved in different teams. We have a detached team working outside the church premises with those young people who do not come in, a café team, a worship team, an audio-visual team, a prayer team and a ministry team. Everyone has a role and a part to play. God has really blessed us and we have grown in numbers, but we still have to work at some of the issues of being a body of Christ and reaching further out into the community. We feel that we have failed if someone

> "We feel that we have failed if someone turns up at Life and can't find a sense of belonging, whoever they are and whatever stage they are at."

turns up at Life and can't find a sense of belonging, whoever they are and whatever stage they are at. Our detached team of workers, both old and young, operates in the car park and around the church chatting and engaging with young people who just happen to have turned up. We have a brilliant team of people working in the café next door to the main meeting, for those young people who have made it over the threshold, but feel intimidated by going into the worship. In the café there are PlayStations, food to buy, drinks, music, pool, and we have the talk from the main worship plugged through into there as well. We hope that through involvement in these teams, or even just having come across a member of these teams, a young person will feel valued, challenged and ultimately will get to a place where they can be discipled.

The best way to finish, is to give you some quotes from some of the young people who attend Life.

'Life is not like any other church I know.' Matt

'Going to the main adult evening congregation isn't going to have the same sense of community . . . with Life I just wanted to be part of it.' Matt (a different one)

'I hope Life isn't a case of them and us (*with the older congregation*). We are all a growing community; we really don't want that to happen.' Gary

'I used to go to church cause I had to, or I just felt obliged. Now I go because I want to go. I feel I can play a part.' Charlotte

Are youth congregations healthy? A Roman Catholic perspective

Avril Baigent

As a Catholic diocesan youth officer, I am continually looking for new ways to make church more accessible to young people. In a church faced with ageing congregations and falling numbers of young Christians, the need to experiment has never been so great. I have been profoundly challenged by Graham Cray's statement in *Mission-shaped Church*:

There is no doubt that youth congregations can meet the needs of a particular (youth) culture. Existing and traditional church seldom realizes its own cultural styles and patterns, and fails to appreciate the large cultural gap that needs to be crossed. Many young people inhabit a different world from that expressed in most churches, and for church to connect gospel and church with them, a fresh expression of church is needed, so that they can find and enjoy authentic Christian community, worship and living.[4]

At the same time, as Bishop Graham has touched upon in Chapter 2, the youth congregation model raises a number of important issues for the Church. In my own spiritual journey, there have been significant adults (including several that would never have thought of themselves as 'youth leaders') who have challenged, supported and encouraged me. These were people that I encountered in diverse parish communities. Geographical boundaries make for varied congregations, whereas special interest or self-selecting groups tend to attract only people like themselves.

There is also the fear that youth congregations make it hard for young people to grow up in their faith. If young people have only ever known what might loosely be termed youth worship, how will they ever feel at home in an adult congregation? Life Teen is an American organization which does great work evangelizing young Catholics primarily through regular Sunday night worship and teaching. They found that they were having to set up groups in universities and colleges because even after Life Teen members stopped being teenagers, they wanted the same kind of very youth-focused worship.

Most importantly, though, the values that young people embody are necessary to the survival of the Church in this country, and only those churches open to this will

❝The value of youth to the Church lies in the typical characteristics of adolescence: heartfelt passion, intolerance of hypocrisy, willingness to experiment, living and breathing secular culture. Take these away from the Church, and we have lost all that propels us forward into new ways of discipleship and mission.❞

be able to reach postmodern people. The value of youth to the Church lies in the typical characteristics of adolescence: heartfelt passion, intolerance of hypocrisy, willingness to experiment, living and breathing secular culture. Take these away from the Church, and we have lost all that propels us forward into new ways of discipleship and mission.

We need each other ... don't we?

Young people need wise adults in their lives to act as mentors and friends. Adults need young people to challenge them, and stop them becoming too cosy and comfortable in their faith. But given the very real struggle to accommodate both groups within one congregation, how can we move forward? To do this, we need to spend some time thinking about how congregations work, and specifically, what the role of young people is within them.

The primary purpose of a congregation is to worship God. Out of this worship come many benefits: being affirmed in your faith, strengthened for the week to come, hearing again the fundamental stories of the faith, and also of how others are living those stories out today. Through this gathering and worship comes a continual process of learning how to be a Christian today. Without a congregation to meet with, we are alone, prey to our own demons, and secure in our own assumptions.

The value of this gathering can, however, be diminished or negated. If the language is archaic or complicated, if the stories have no relevance, or if the ritual makes no sense, then the gathering is reduced to a dutiful presence. If the worship exists in a sacred bubble, having no connection to the secular world, then the gathering becomes a holy enclave or a social occasion. If a congregation is to function properly, it needs a full set of working parts. It needs a shared experience of God, and a shared language to describe that experience. It needs a common understanding of mission. It needs a set of founding stories, both scriptural and more recent. And it needs both wise leadership, and prophetic, challenging voices.

A congregation also has to balance tradition and innovation, looking both to the past and the future. Without a sense of history, there is no connection to the hundreds of years of Christian experience and reflection. All discoveries must be made anew, and all mistakes remade. Even language must be reinvented, to a certain extent. Without a regular structure, people become uneasy, and can be distracted by what's new, rather than drawn into it. This applies just as much to teenagers as to anyone else. With so much that's uncertain in their world (ranging from the global issue of terrorism to the much more personal issues of family breakdown), once they find a structure that they like, they can be pretty rigid about sticking to it.

On the other hand, without innovation, a congregation can become stale and out of date. The Christian message must speak challengingly to people's lives, and must continue to call them out of their comfort zone. It must speak to people where they really are, breaking through any protective sense of piety. In order to fulfil its mission, the congregation has to engage with society as it is. The founding stories have to be recast in ways that are comprehensible to today's audience, without losing their historical truths. Our church communities have to be places of safety, but they have also to be open to the perilous influence of the Holy Spirit.

> Our church communities have to be places of safety, but they have also to be open to the perilous influence of the Holy Spirit.

How do young people fit in to our congregations? Unfortunately, the way we integrate young people into our communities tends to represent either end of the extremes presented above.

Let's just ignore them until they grow up

The reaction of most church communities to the challenge of adolescence is to ignore it. In these communities once children stop being cute, they are valued only to the extent that they can behave like adults. They are given adult roles such as reading and playing with the music group. Membership of the adult community happens at an

> The reaction of most church communities to the challenge of adolescence is to ignore it. In these communities once children stop being cute, they are valued only to the extent that they can behave like adults.

indeterminate age – anything from confirmation/adult baptism as a teenager to being asked to join the parish council in middle age – and often without any ritual notice. Youth is only valued statistically, in a 'bums on pews' way, and any concession to teenage spirituality is tokenistic.

The value of this approach is that young people grow up well-versed in the traditions and language of the faith. In an uncertain world, there is a lot of certainty here. If the spark of faith has been lit along the way, the young person will have learnt a certain spiritual discipline and encountered older role models to help in their journey. However, they may not have been encouraged to relate their faith to the world they live in, leading to a kind of 'splitting' between 'spiritual' and 'secular' life. They also have no way of passing the good news on to their peers, as they have no suitable language. Many feel that their faith does not belong to them personally, but has been passed on by their parents, or through schooling.

To separate or not to separate? That is the question

The alternative approach is for young people to be separate from the main community. Sometimes this happens when they meet the kind of barriers outlined in the first approach, and they go outside the structure to find their own place. Sometimes it is imposed by the community, which wants to have vibrant youth ministry but is not capable of dealing with the results. In a separate group young people have a lot of freedom to express their faith. They can be creative in drawing on their own culture. They can use their own language, technology and concepts. Such groups also start out with great missionary zeal (although this can die out as they get older!), and because they are far more culturally relevant have a lot more success in reaching other young people. The problems here are the reverse of the first model. These young people do not know the language and practices of the adult community, and it can be very difficult for them to find a spiritual home as they leave adolescence behind. Without careful leadership, these groups can also run into extremism of one kind or another.

In many of our churches, the first approach has dominated for years. While the saying 'children should be seen and not heard' disappeared from parenting years ago, it's still very much in evidence in church circles. Youth congregations are a reaction to this – a way of giving young people a voice and a way of expressing their spirituality. But in neither of these models is the gift of youth present to the adult congregation. To be truly effective, young people must be allowed to express their authentic spirituality in the middle of the adult congregation often enough that relationships can be built, and the creative tension starts to make its presence felt.

> ❝Young people must be allowed to express their authentic spirituality in the middle of the adult congregation often enough that relationships can be built, and the creative tension starts to make its presence felt.❞

What next?

How, then, can we move forward? There are no easy answers here. In fact, no answers at all – but instead two justifications for persevering in trying to find ways in which both young people and adults can worship and grow in their faith together. The first is theological, and the second arises out of good youth-work practice. In Paul's first letter to the Corinthians, he was writing to a radically divided congregation, so far from being a united community that they actually had lawsuits out against each other. In a very well-known passage, he urges them to think of themselves as a human body:

> God arranged the members in the body, each one of them, as he chose. If all were a single member, where would the body be? . . . Now you are the body of Christ and individually members of it.
>
> (1 Corinthians 12.18, 19, 27)

This is very much unity in diversity. All the parts of the body are necessary and different. Indeed, the thought of a body consisting only of eyes or feet is grotesque. Paul also reminds us that what we consider to be the weaker parts of the body are the ones we take special care over. It is such a familiar passage that it is easy to be blasé or pious about it, not recognizing the real challenge implicit here. What would it mean for us to take seriously the idea that each part of the Body of Christ is different but equally necessary?

There is a Catholic theological term which is useful here: communio. It arose from thinking about the Trinity as a co-equal, co-dependent, co-responsible relationship of love. When applied to communities, it means legitimate diversity, subsidiarity and co-responsibility. Unity in diversity allows for creativity and gives freedom for experimentation. Co-responsibility implies that each member must take his or her own part in the mission of the Church. Co-dependency reminds us that if one part of the community is hurt or lost, all are affected. Co-equality re-addresses the natural tendency to Pharisaism in religious communities. The community is one which is open to the promptings of the Holy Spirit and recognizes the gifts of all.

In this model, each person is valued for their contribution to the work of mission Jesus left to his disciples according to their abilities, rather than their status. It not only restores young people to their place in the community, but values other forgotten members: the housebound person dedicated to a life of prayer; the sick, teaching about patience and endurance; those who have suffered heavy losses, representing hope shining in the darkness. It recognizes, as in Paul's description, that there is unity in difference, but it is also a calling to a radical life of discipleship, lived out according to each person's circumstances. It requires the wisdom and experience of adults and the passion and clear-sightedness of young people, held in a holy tension. It is also a terrifying model, requiring humility, patience, a willingness to listen and creativity. It demands that all parties lay down their agenda and their positions of power. It is not a quick fix.

Questions for discussion

1. What part do young people play in the life of your church at the moment? What opportunities are they given to serve? How do adult members of the church view them? What is their understanding of their own role and importance?

2. How can a group develop from running a youth service to becoming a youth congregation?

3. Avril outlined some of the pros and cons both of all ages worshipping together and of youth congregations. Which of these resonated with

you? How can we overcome some of the negative aspects of each model?

4. What would it mean for us to take seriously the idea that each part of the Body of Christ is different but all are equally necessary?

5. Do we really want young people as part of our church? If they are in a separate service or congregation, how can we encourage them to feel a genuine sense of belonging to the wider church?

Further resources

Further reading on youth congregations

Craig Abbot, 'What's the link between "youth church" and "adult church"?' in Mark Montgomery (ed.), *Young People and Worship*, Church House Publishing, 2007.

Discusses the pros and cons of youth congregations and lists questions you need to consider if you are thinking of setting up a youth congregation.

Graham Cray, *Youth Congregations and the Emerging Church*, Grove Booklet Ev57, Grove Books, 1998.

Michael Moynagh, 'Good practice is not what it used to be: accumulating wisdom for fresh expressions of church', in Steven Croft (ed.), *The Future of the Parish System: Shaping the Church of England in the 21st century*, Church House Publishing, 2006.

Web sites

Eden: www.edenzone.com

Life: sucs.org/~ct/life/index.php

Pulse: www.christchurchyouth.com

The Fresh Expressions web site carries details of youth congregations throughout the UK: www.freshexpressions.org.uk

6 Young people outside the Church

In many churches the reality is that the young people the church would 'like' to work with are at best 'alien', at worst frightening, and miles away from the church culture we know and like. These projects describe young people who would traditionally be described as hard to reach. But it is these young people who are in the majority, nationally. They don't go to church, in many cases their parents don't and didn't go to church. These projects show a process of 'pre-evangelism' and new approaches to honest dialogue that is needed when you want to work with such young people.

Grafted project, Scottish Borders
Paul Little

Grafted (www.grafted.co.uk) is a project that exists to provide young people with opportunities to explore their potential in life using a holistic approach. We achieve this through a blend of contemporary youth work, outdoor activities and enabling the development of relevant expressions of church where appropriate.

How Grafted started

Since winter 2003 I have been running Grafted working with young people in the Scottish Borders. Previously I had been working as part of the In2venture outdoors activity team at Whithaugh Park, Newcastleton, where thousands of young people come to take part in a variety of activities. As each session only lasts for a maximum of two hours including safety instruction and the opportunity to try the activity, there was little opportunity for sharing the good news of Jesus. I began to see the need for something that combined the outdoor activities that young people love with the challenge of the gospel.

Within six months of arriving at Whithaugh Park, I began to build a 50-metre underground tunnel system in an old quarry on the site. This consists of six underground chambers connected by tunnels that you crawl through. I called this tunnel system the Walk of Life and it has become a place that we use for challenging young people about the existence of God. I am excited that over 900 young people took part in the Walk of Life in the first year and the number has now risen to about 1,500 people per year. Our focus is on providing this activity for unchurched young people and the issues we raise are:

- Did we evolve or are we created?

- Why and how do we value people?

- How do we make choices?

- Is there an afterlife?

- Is there a difference between faith and belief?

Schools are the main users and we have had a lot of good responses to the issues we raise. I have done my share of school assemblies and found that either I was not gifted in this area or secondary school assemblies are the most hostile place on the earth for talking about Jesus. The opposite is true in the Walk of Life: secondary-aged young people really engage with the activity and the issues that it raises. The tunnel system is very challenging and a good activity in its own right. When you add in group work with discussion and a few provocative statements from the instructors, the young people leave the tunnels buzzing. The feedback we receive nearly always includes positive comments about the learning experience as well as the physical challenge. We are currently at the early stages of discussing a proposal to build a second Walk of Life on a double-decker bus so that it can be fully mobile.

After developing the Walk of Life I began to develop a mobile activity trailer. This trailer is a 13-metre-long bouldering wall and an archery range. The trailer also carries go-karts, problem-solving equipment and a Giro-seat. Using this trailer, I am able to work with groups just about anywhere.

Vision

For me, vision is the starting point for everything that Grafted does. We have to realize that if we are going to ask God to speak to us, we had better be

> **❝**For me, vision is the starting point for everything that Grafted does. We have to realize that if we are going to ask God to speak to us, we had better be prepared to accept the answer, and even turn away from what we are currently doing if necessary. Asking God for vision is really serious stuff!**❞**

prepared to accept the answer, and even turn away from what we are currently doing if necessary. Asking God for vision is really serious stuff!

When I was two and a half years into my contract as youth worker for Whithaugh Park, God gave me a new vision for Grafted. I took this vision to the people that employed me, In2venture, Church Army and the Barnabas Trust. They all supported the vision and agreed to support the new work.

This current vision for Grafted has grown out of my experience of youth work at Whithaugh Park, Scottish Borders and also out of a longer-term personal vision that I hold to reach out to excluded young people and to offer hope to the hopeless.

Reasons for rethinking our previous way of working

Any mission and evangelism needs to be informed and shaped by the mission context in which you are working. Young people are an incredibly diverse and ever-changing people group, with very varied and individual needs that shift like sand in the desert. My experience is that young people seem to be drawn to something if it is fun and/or different. My experience of youth work in the Borders and within our local village has taught me that it can be very hard to work with a young person for more than a couple of years. I believe there are a few reasons for this. The first is that young people do not tend to choose to stay with a youth project very long. Young people like to be able to choose almost weekly where they will go and what they will do, and don't seem to feel as if they need to commit to or support a project.

Another problem is that you can get a 'gang' attachment to the youth work. When this happens, a group of young people see it as their own and only people who are 'in' with that gang tend to come. This can make for good numbers until some 'key person' leaves and suddenly you are halfway through the programme and everybody's gone.

One solution to these problems is to put on lots of short-term work rather than long-term programmes. This demands less commitment from the young people, and also allows for the fallouts and relationship changes that happen. To assist the Church in reaching such a broad mission field as young people, I decided that Grafted needed a very wide net. That is why I am currently developing three main areas of work.

Helping others in their outreach to young people

We have a mobile trailer and activity centre which is available for working alongside existing outreach to young people. Groups find it harder and harder to get insurance and risk assessments sorted for events and activities. We bring all of those plus five mobile activities to events so that fun and outreach can happen using outdoor activities as a tool. We have received requests for the trailer from all over the UK and from Ireland too.

Reaching out to young people directly

Grafted works with young people in our local area by mixing outdoor activities with a more traditional approach to youth work. We have the use of a community room and some pool and video equipment and use the outdoor activities during the year. Last year we ran Activity Alpha where we talked about faith to young people as they dangled 10 metres up in the air on a climbing rope! We also used archery to help us to explain sin and wrongdoing.

Alongside Mike McCliester (Selkirk Baptist Church) and Keith Scott (Books Plus), I am one of the founder members of SoulSpan, which aims to provide an opportunity for young people to develop and experience a fresh expression of church within the Borders. At the time of writing SoulSpan events take place every six to eight weeks and young people lead the worship. Long-term, SoulSpan could facilitate the development of a network of fresh expressions of church that are relevant to the young people who attend. SoulSpan currently attracts an average of about 120 young people, who travel from all over the Borders to attend.

Working with young people at risk

Over the past 18 months a lot of my time has been devoted to reaching out to young people who have been excluded and are at risk. When I arrived in the

Borders I began to attend the Borders Voluntary Youth Work Forum (BVYWF). This forum is made up of a group of project leaders and workers mainly from the voluntary sector, but also includes some statutory workers, such as police and local government youth leaders. This has been my main area of networking and I have made some great friends and contacts.

Since 2003 I have also been working with young people who are at high risk of offending, as a result of an invitation from the Scottish Borders Youth Offending Service (YOS) which came through the BVYWF. The work began because of a meeting with the head of the new Fast Track Team. He was setting up this new part of the service and asked me to work with him in developing some ideas.

Using outdoor activity training we have seen some great results and changes in the lives of the young people. These changes were very apparent from the start. During a 10-week course of Friday evening kayak and white-water skills training, only one of the young people attending was picked up by the police, for one offence. Before the course began, all of the young people had been regularly offending. The 10-week programme proved that this area of work is well worth further development.

None of these young people were attending school, some were in full-time care and most had never achieved any qualifications. The YOS was very satisfied with the course and its results. It was pleased and also surprised that the young people were committed enough to finish the 10-week course, and asked us to lead four such courses in the following year.

The future and the hurdles we foresee

The Window of Time is the next development of the work with young people at risk. This will involve a whole year of work with a group of ten very high-risk young people. Our vision is to turn these young people into future leaders. We aim to help them to reach their own potential as leaders and people through training them as outdoor instructors and coaches.

Finding the right staff to work on such a project may be a challenge. The amount of travelling that we do is always on the increase and travel costs seem to keep rising, so I may need to curb some of the work we do at greater distance or pass this work onto another part of In2venture. I have set up a steering group help me think through future development.

I feel that one of the challenges ahead for Grafted is to play its part in reaching out to a generation that has little or no knowledge of God. I believe the way ahead is to partner with others who can offer church for young people, but for some I expect to have to provide resources for discipleship and fellowship and help them to discover faith in Christ.

❝I feel that one of the challenges ahead for Grafted is to play its part in reaching out to a generation that has little or no knowledge of God. I believe the way ahead is to partner with others who can offer church for young people, but for some I expect to have to provide resources for discipleship and fellowship and help them to discover faith in Christ.❞

A reflection on inter-faith work

Andrew Smith

How do you speak of truth to people who have a totally different understanding of truth? How do you share your faith with people who already have a faith and will never come near any sort of church event? These are issues facing churches up and down the country as they grapple with what mission looks like among people of different faiths. These are also issues that

❝How do you speak of truth to people who have a totally different understanding of truth? How do you share your faith with people who already have a faith and will never come near any sort of church event?❞

growing numbers of Christians face as the diversity of the world becomes ever more real in their own local area.

I was chatting to a group of Muslim lads at a school over a period of weeks and got increasingly frustrated with where the conversations were going. Every time the Bible was mentioned they rejected it because it was written by a number of hands, had been translated (and corrupted, so they believed) and, to them, was full of contradictions. They also constantly questioned my very understanding of God. How can God have a son when he has no wife? How could I believe in the Trinity when it made no sense? I felt frustrated at their reluctance (or refusal) to ask similar tough questions about their own faith and the Qur'an. They saw the simplicity of one book in one language revealed by one God to one prophet as a beauty which demonstrated its truth. In the Bible I saw the complexity of many writers all finding consistency on the message, and the divine mystery of the Trinity as revealing God as beyond human invention. In that complexity I found truth. But trying to find ways of speaking and hearing truth seemed beyond us.

Then one day I came up with a new set of rules for our discussions to try to help us pick a way through. I told the guys that to start with I would trust that they believed the Qur'an to be true and invite them to tell me of its riches and the blessings I might find within its pages. I might want to ask questions to understand their beliefs better but I wouldn't undermine their essential starting point. Then we would turn the tables. They would trust that I believe the Bible to be the word of God and allow me to tell them of the riches and blessings to be found there. Again, they could ask questions to get better understanding but they wouldn't question that fundamental belief.

At the time I didn't realize that I was entering the labyrinthine world of Christian–Muslim dialogue. It was a pragmatic response to an opportunity. Here were guys interested in what I believed (and keen to convert me to Islam) but with whom it was hard to find even basic ground rules that would allow a discussion. That experience set me to exploring and engaging in the world of Christian–Muslim dialogue, but with a passion for mission.

> ❝There are many folk for whom the words 'mission' and 'dialogue' are diametrically opposed – you can only do one or the other. Yet it seems to me that the two are inextricably linked.❞

There are many folk for whom the words 'mission' and 'dialogue' are diametrically opposed – you can only do one or the other. Yet it seems to me that the two are inextricably linked. Surely any mission has to treat the hearer with love and respect, which involves listening to them and getting to know them. This is dialogue: being willing to listen as well as speak. But any dialogue is bound to be some witness simply by our being together. The way we treat our Muslim interlocutors will witness to our faith either for good or ill. How we listen to them and the words we use will quite naturally continue the process of witness.

But is witnessing in this way mission?

Mission clearly contains a proclamation of the gospel and is normally considered to include a call to be a disciple of Jesus. But is that all mission is? And is that the starting point of mission or one step in a long, and often convoluted, journey? Can there be other expressions of mission? According to Luke, Jesus' declaration of his mission comes before his calling of the disciples in Luke 5. Back in Luke 4 we get the account of Jesus reading from the book of Isaiah and claiming the prophecy for himself. This prophecy speaks of someone who will preach good news, proclaim freedom for prisoners, recovery of sight for the blind, release for the oppressed and proclaim the year of the Lord's favour (Luke 4.17-21). When Jesus thought of mission he wasn't just thinking of calling disciples. We see this worked out later on in Luke 17 when he heals 10 lepers. When they cry out for help Jesus doesn't check their theology, he just meets their needs. It's only when one returns to thank Jesus we discover he was a Samaritan. And Jesus' final words to him? 'Get up and go on your way; your faith has made you well' (Luke 17.19). Not much of a proclamation of the gospel or call to discipleship. So mission embraces the proclamation of the gospel, a call to discipleship and the working out of Christ's commands, and following his example here on earth.

Some of my early encounters with those Muslim lads could be quite fraught. Sadly, lots of encounters between people with strongly held beliefs lead to conflict. Yet Jesus calls us to be peacemakers (Matthew 5.9) and calls us to a radical approach to conflict resolution (Luke 6.27-36). In a world where terrorists are causing all Muslims to be seen as a potential threat, what should our response be? I believe simply that it should be to love those whom some would call 'our enemies' simply by virtue of their faith. When I looked back on my encounters with those lads I could see that there wasn't much love lost in the early days. Setting a framework which demanded that I listen to them was a small step to show that I loved them as they were. I wanted to find out about their faith because it mattered to them, not so that I could prove them wrong. Being a peacemaker, learning to love became part of my mission with those young people.

I believe dialogue becomes part of the mission of the Church because of the call to be peacemakers. This is a mission to bring peace between people, a

> This is a mission to bring peace between people, a mission to love those the world rejects, a mission to bless those who curse some things we love, a mission to turn the other cheek.

mission to love those the world rejects, a mission to bless those who curse some things we love, a mission to turn the other cheek. Yet by finding a structure for this mission it becomes a place where truth can be heard. And in the subsequent events I've run that bring together Christian and Muslim young people I've learnt that they love hearing each other's faith stories. I've seen Christians ask about Muslim prayer and I've seen Muslims listen intently as Christians talk about their faith in Jesus. Truth shared.

If you want a mission where the only result is conversion, this probably isn't what you're looking for. If, however, you want a mission that attempts to bless those of other faiths while finding space to speak of the hope we have within us (1 Peter 3.15), this might just help.

Questions for discussion

1. Often we find the hardest mission field to be on our own doorsteps. Which groups of local young people are on the margins in your area?

2. Does it take a certain type of youth worker to work with young people on the margins? What characteristics are essential in this type of work?

3. Are there ways in which the church can work alongside other organizations or statutory bodies in your area (for example, in inter-faith dialogue)?

4. Do we really want young people on the margins to be part of our church? In what ways does the church need to show its commitment to these young people and those who work with them?

Further resources

Grafted:www.grafted.co.uk

See also the Frontier Youth Trust web site: www.fyt.org.uk

Frontier Youth Trust publish numerous resources, which are listed on the web site.

Also see David Booker, 'Ignorance is bliss? Young Christians living in a multi-faith society' in D. Booker (ed.), *Young People and Mission*, Church House Publishing, 2007.

7 Creative approaches to prayer and sacraments

Youth ministry has often led the way in reworking traditional forms of Christian worship and revamping them for the new millennium. Projects that combine the ancient with the modern somehow connect deeply with people who are searching for authenticity and depth. Examples include the St Paul's Labyrinth, which was created by London alternative worship groups, the use of sacred spaces, Critical Mass and 24-7 prayer. You could argue that the Critical Mass case study could just as well belong in the chapter on congregationally based projects, but it is included here because of its unashamed reworking of a traditional Eucharist.

24-7 prayer, international project
Ian Nicholson

The history and background

There are nightclubs and nightclubs. In some city centres there are the ultra-modern, subtly lit temples of cool where the beautiful people gather. Bojanglez in Guildford is the other type! 'Bo's' has a lingering smell of stale beer and the dance floor sticks to your shoes with the residue of the previous night's drinking. There are shards of glass scattered in the corners and the lights are always dimmed to hide the damp patches, peeling paintwork and appalling décor.

Bojanglez is not the sort of place you would choose to launch a vibrant youth mission movement. In fact the imposing cathedral just a mile away would be many people's first choice. However, 400 young people from all over the UK did make it to Guildford on a February night in 2000 to launch a commitment to continual prayer. Many were from Chichester, where 100 or so in the Warehouse youth congregation had just completed three months of non-stop

24-7 prayer. Warehouse was one of the first prominent examples of mission-motivated youth churches, which were exploring how to build Christian communities within youth culture.

However, the Warehouse crowd were certainly not a group of supercharged dedicated, vibrant intercessors. They were, like most of us, inconsistent and lethargic about prayer. In response to a challenge to pray non-stop for a month they decorated a dedicated room to be an interactive artistic prayer area, committed to complete the month, started praying – and were totally taken by surprise!

As the month developed there was a tangible sense of God's presence in the prayer room. Hundreds of names of non-believing friends were scribbled on walls, dramatic artistic statements emerged and people's lives were transformed. Pete Greig, the leader of Warehouse, would say that the launch of 24-7 (www.24-7prayer.com) was a God-inspired accident and they had no idea where this small step would lead.

Through email and word of mouth the stories from the Chichester prayer room spread to other groups of students and young people and the next idea was to launch a year of non-stop prayer through a chain of UK prayer rooms. That was why people came to Bojanglez. At a key part of the evening a huge shout of 'Come on' went up to kick the year off. The first week of non-stop prayer was in a small United Reformed Church in Guildford. I wrote at the end of that week,

> It is no exaggeration to say that the last six years have been a phenomenon, a time of constant surprise and bewildering change – with very little of it planned! Similar groups such as Conta Corriente (Counter Current) in Spain, Freakstock in Germany and Interact in Sweden let out their own 'Come on' cries and the movement has spread across Europe. After six years there is a movement of prayer emerging across North America, New Zealand and South Africa. That one prayer room has multiplied into thousands in over 60 nations. This has not been a slickly planned campaign but simply groups of friends and a website, www.24-7prayer.com, spreading the word. There have been prayer rooms in university campuses, festivals, bars, police stations, cathedrals, the US naval academy and a brewery!

What is a 24-7 prayer room?

> A typical 24-7 prayer room is simple and accessible, to those of many years' faith and those of none, to the young, students, children, but also families and the elderly. The room can be full of noisy, card-carrying charismatics one hour and then host a group of contemplatives the next.

The prayer rooms remain at the heart of this movement. A typical 24-7 prayer room is simple and accessible, to those of many years' faith and those of none, to the young, students, children, but also families and the elderly. The room can be full of noisy, card-carrying charismatics one hour and then host a group of contemplatives the next. The Reading Boiler Room regularly has Christians of all flavours, business people, skateboarders, prostitutes, drug addicts and goths, meeting to connect with God through prayer.

24-7 and young people

The 24-7 prayer movement has grown within a vision for mission-oriented

> The 24-7 prayer movement has grown within a vision for mission-oriented church in youth culture. It is as much about mission, justice, serving the poor and building church as personal blessing and renewal.

church in youth culture. This context has had a big impact on the movement. It has given a determination that prayer will not remain a ghetto activity of the Christian community. It is as much about mission, justice, serving the poor and building church as personal blessing and renewal. The determination is that it moves participants beyond Christian consumerism to lasting community change, particularly in building church that reaches the young.

Within a year of the launch of the first prayer room teams of young people and students were heading out to some of the 'high places of youth culture' to 'play, pray and obey'. At the invitation of the Anglican chaplaincy on Ibiza a team set up a prayer room in the centre of San Antonio, which, notoriously in the UK, was the main 'sun, sex and sangria' destination for British tourists. The impact was, again, beyond all expectations as the teams prayed for people, DJed, cleaned beaches and lived at the heart of the clubbing community. British newspapers ran positive stories, Radio 1 profiled the team and Channel 4 commissioned an hour-long documentary called *God Bless Ibiza*.

The teams haven't been a flash-in-the-pan summer experience. After five years of summer prayer rooms a young family have moved to live on the island with the slogan 'building, not visiting' – expressing their long-term commitment to building a 24-7 community. Other teams have been to Ayia Napa in Cyprus and to Tenerife and have worked with student communities in Belgrade, drug addicts in Russia, young Balkan holidaymakers in Macedonia, backpackers in Thailand, surfers in Mexico, and on the fringe at the Edinburgh festival. The stories from each summer are often astounding and express church at its incarnational best, engaged at the heart of the community.

The third arm to the development of 24-7 has been the emergence of 24-7 praying communities, known as Boiler Rooms. Inspired by the monastic traditions of holistic community living, Boiler Rooms combine a rhythm of prayer and a heart for justice with hospitality, creativity and mission, particularly to the poor. Andy Freeman, who led the Reading Boiler Room,

> Inspired by the monastic traditions of holistic community living, Boiler Rooms combine a rhythm of prayer and a heart for justice with hospitality, creativity and mission, particularly to the poor.

commented that for many years he was an Anglican youth worker wanting to work with needy young people and feeling that something was missing. Within six months of opening a prayer room he had had more impact than in those previous years. The Boiler Room became a magnet to marginalized young people. Andy found it particularly moving when the parents of one young lad who had died of a drug overdose asked that all money given in his memory should go to the Boiler Room as 'for the last six months of his life they were his family'. I took a group of five or six youth workers to spend a day in the Boiler Room and several independently commented that this was their idea of church!

The growth of 24-7 is seen by many as a key opportunity in enabling a new generation to encounter God, rethink church and mobilize to reach beyond traditional boundaries to impact the unchurched. Perhaps it's a good thing it didn't emerge from a manual, committee or conference! In 2005 Pete Greig commented that 24-7 is now much more than simply a prayer movement: it is a mission and community movement which prays a lot.

Hundreds of young people would see 24-7 as connecting with their aspirations and instincts as Christians. They want to experience God, they want to make a difference in society, but they also want to build communities of change. The attraction of the 24-7 model is its fluidity and accessibility. It is easy to adopt and adapt and any group of friends with a room, a CD player and a kettle can 'give it a go'. There is little bureaucracy to encounter and there should be few objections from the Church to people praying!

In some situations 24-7 is a renewal agent within existing churches and denominations. The Methodists, Salvation Army and Pioneer group of churches have all run their own year of prayer.

In other contexts 24-7 is a uniting agent, fluid and flexible enough to combine churches with a common vision for a town or city. Many of the best prayer rooms are partnerships between a number of churches, and London ran its own year of prayer as part of the lead-in to the Soul in the City mission in 2004.

In yet more places 24-7 is a launch pad for mission – prayer rooms are accessible to all and a non-threatening way for people of all backgrounds to encounter God through prayer. The model of setting up rooms at the centre of the community, praying for people's needs and sharing the gospel from a context of service and friendship is generally well received in comparison to more confrontational or impersonal models of evangelism.

> ❝The model of setting up rooms at the centre of the community, praying for people's needs and sharing the gospel from a context of service and friendship is generally well received.❞

Future vision of 24-7

So where do we hope that all this will lead? At the heart is the conviction that expressions of church that connect with society and particularly young people and students need to multiply in a new way. It is inevitable that the 24-7 values will be expressed in many different ways.

The aspiration is that Boiler Room centres will emerge across the UK and Europe and draw together existing churches to pray and engage in mission. Where there are insufficient resources to enable a Boiler Room to be sustained, smaller missional communities, supported within existing churches, could still look to live by similar values. The prayer room model also has huge potential in planting projects at the heart of unchurched communities, whether geographically or among particular cultural groups.

Future challenges for 24-7

The challenge for 24-7 is to enable these rapidly emerging initiatives to be sustained. There is a considerable need for training and mentoring of young leaders. There needs to be a proliferation of older leaders who are able to support and provide wisdom without dampening the life and vibrancy of the groups.

There also needs to be the allocation of significant financial resources to empower and develop mission projects, Boiler Rooms and training programmes. Across Europe there is a depressingly familiar story of incredibly promising youth initiatives which start well, are applauded from the sidelines for a while but then falter as leaders burn out or lose heart through lack of dedicated support, training and finance for the long haul.

If I can close a bit more personally: I have been writing this paper in Dresden and have had constant background noise as young 24-7 leaders gather from all over Germany for a weekend of friendship and to dream about where God wants to take them. The enthusiasm is tangible and the stories are encouraging. In Britain 24-7 leaders gathered in Leeds from all over the UK and Northern Ireland to share ideas and dream together. This is being duplicated all over Europe, North America and in Australasia.

I am approaching 50 and have given most of my energy of the past 20 years in wanting to see expressions of church emerge which have a lasting impact on the young. I still see it as the priority issue for the Church. I believe that God is opening many doors and the energy, passion, maturity and vision of young Christians is remarkable. To me, 24-7 has been the most surprising and spontaneous movement I have ever encountered.

It is well known that the church is struggling to attract young people and students and, although it has now broadened, the original slogan for 24-7 was 'turning the tide in youth culture'. This transformation will take much more than a few exciting youth events and initiatives. It will take a focused and dedicated allocation of resources from the whole Church. It will also take some fresh and bold thinking.

It is imperative that those of us who have been around a while take notice of movements like 24-7. If we can give of our experience and resources to enable these fledgling initiatives to grow and become established – even if we don't fully understand them – it will be a lasting legacy and a huge sign of hope for the future of faith and the Church in our nation.

Critical Mass, Peterborough
Tim Sledge

The history and background

'Do you want me to carry the Jesus Stick, Father?'

The question came from a lanky 15-year-old, two minutes before the start of the Sung Eucharist in a rural church in Northamptonshire. Even before the procession had started he looked utterly bored and disinterested in what was going on. After I had prevented him from potting an imaginary pool ball with the so-called 'Jesus Stick', off we set down the long chancel to a wrist-slittingly dull and turgid hymn. Inside I was smiling at this teenager who was now solemnly leading the procession as crucifer. By the time I reached the altar, my heart was sinking at the quality of the worship. But just as I was sitting thinking there must be more to worship than this, I saw the bored teenager who had now propped the Jesus Stick up against the side wall. Was he thinking what I was thinking? The simple truth was that this worship – important as it was to the assembled faithful gathering – made little or no impact on the couple of teenagers there.

'The Lord is here,' I proclaimed faithfully. I could almost hear the young guy muttering back his response, 'You could have fooled me.'

The vision of Critical Mass

After this experience I discussed with Revd Paul Niemic, the Peterborough diocesan youth officer, what there was in the more middle-of-the-road and catholic churches for the few young people who faithfully came, whether through choice or coercion. Nothing, we concluded. OK, there were a few loyal church choirs, the odd music group, a small number of youth groups and a minority who were happy to be part of the established service. But for the vast majority there was nothing that they could connect with.

The larger, mostly evangelical, churches all seemed to have more established youth groups, access to events like Soul Survivor and New Wine or their own youth cells and Bible study groups. But my heart went out to the 'Jesus Stick' teenager and dozens and dozens like him scattered around a large number of our churches in the diocese, for whom worship made little or no connection with their lives.

So Critical Mass was born. Paul and I worked well together because we brought different gifts – the ability to organize a large-scale youth event, and some liturgical know-how and creativity. Both were vital ingredients for the venture, and I thank God for our different gifts, which complemented each other and provided exactly what was needed for this worship.

The liturgy and structure of Critical Mass

We kept the structure of the Eucharist as our template but aimed to breathe new understanding into it. The essential eucharistic structure has worked for the vast part of two millennia, so we weren't going to tinker with it now! In some ways, we saw this as an extended Eucharist with opportunities for young people to feed on word and sacrament, to gain a fresh understanding of the liturgy and to be renewed in their worship of God. This is an outline of how we developed the sessions.

> ❝We saw this as an extended Eucharist with opportunities for young people to feed on word and sacrament, to gain a fresh understanding of the liturgy and to be renewed in their worship of God.❞

The venue

For the first Critical Mass, we chose a large Anglo-Catholic church in Northampton which had movable chairs and a willingness to let us do whatever we wanted. The building was gifted to us for the day.

The layout

If you read Richard Giles's books *Re-pitching the Tent* and *Creating Uncommon Worship*, you begin to get an idea of the potential for letting the church building speak of the glory of God. He examines how to re-order a church so that the building and environment play as much of a part in helping people into a living encounter with God as the worship itself. For young people, environment and feel is very important. So we laid out the church as in the diagram on page 80, offering a different focus for each of the parts of the eucharistic liturgy.

The gathering

The service had a 'soft start'. As the young people gathered there were quality refreshments, a chance to meet friends and time to get used to what was probably quite an unfamiliar environment compared with their own churches. There was music in the background and a variety of images were projected on to three screens. During the service we used these screens for words, still images and close-up shots of the 'high points' of the liturgy. There was a balti dish with incense gently smoking away throughout the service, which provided a very effective haze to shoot coloured light through. We had hoped to create an atmospheric environment for worship, a sacred space and a time of quiet, but the reality was that gathering, finding friends and creating a safe place to soak up the atmosphere were much more important.

The Welcome

We introduced the theme of the service and put the young people at ease. Then we handed over to the musicians to teach everyone some new music.

The service had a distinct start with a hymn and a procession of crucifer (not the same guy with the Jesus Stick!), together with key symbols we were going to use through the service – three crosses, a purple robe, a crown of thorns and a large Bible. These were then placed in the centre of the worship space.

The Confession

The Confession was done with words and actions. Someone led a simple responsive prayer over some background music. Around the three crosses we had placed nails, hammers and small strips of red ribbon. As music played, everyone was invited to 'nail their sins to the cross'. We then sang a penitential song. For the Absolution, the crosses were replaced with three clean ones – marking our cleansing and forgiveness.

The Ministry of the Word

We focused on a single Gospel reading, based on the theme of the service. Rather than a sermon, we 'broke open' the word by splitting into three groups, each encouraged by a leader. One group wrote prayers based on the theme of the reading. One group was invited to write a 'manifesto' or credal statement and the third was invited to look at images of Christ which we had gathered from various sources and were scattered all over the church. We asked this group to discuss which pictures they liked or could identify with and why they were drawn to or repelled by a particular image.

After about 15 minutes, we gathered the worship together and invited the groups to share their images, to speak out their credal statements, and to lead the prayers with sung response.

The Peace

The Peace was a break for five minutes just to allow everyone to mix a bit more and to move around, an important break in what was quite a long act of worship.

The Ministry of the Sacrament

As we had laid out the worship space with a Table of the Word and Table of the Sacrament, we invited everyone (200 at the first event) to gather around the altar. Because the Eucharistic Prayer is visual as well as verbal we wanted people to be caught up praying with their eyes open and reliving the words of the Last Supper. To help with this we had a video camera enabling us to project on to the screen a close-up of the elevation and blessing of the elements to draw everyone closer in to the action.

We invited everyone who wanted to to receive communion. Many did, and those who were not confirmed still saw this as an important rite of passage, and received a blessing as they would have done on a Sunday.

The Blessing and Dismissal

The Dismissal is often the unsung climax of the liturgy. We felt this was an important time for the young people to be equipped to feed a hungry and broken world as they had been fed with the broken body of Jesus in word and sacrament.

For the Dismissal, we provided 'take-away bags' full of ideas about how they could feed the world. We had information on fair trade, some chocolate, some stories of things which they could do, all as part of taking Jesus to the world. Finally, we finished the whole thing with pizzas and garlic bread.

Music

For our first service we used CJM, a professional Roman Catholic renewal band. They were a group of musicians who created their own music, used the latest renewal songs and were 'liturgically savvy'. They knew and understood the shape of the service and were able to understand the flexibility of the liturgy. They were also able to cope when we had a few glitches. Since then we have used local music groups, and have spent time talking through what happens in the liturgy and why, and teaching them some modern, mostly Roman Catholic, settings of music for the Mass. At the most recent Critical Mass, we set up in a local church secondary school. The musicians were from the music department in the school. They worked with us, took our suggestions and rewrote some music to fit with the liturgy themselves!

The music was a mix of traditional hymns, some well-known choruses, some new renewal songs and the Mass setting. This meant that at the start of the service, as part of the gathering, there was a chance to learn some new songs and that put most people on an equal footing. Everyone was learning something new!

Publicity

We now have a logo and a 'brand identity'. We pushed the service hard with individual invitations to middle- and high-church parishes and publicized it through schools and other networks. Both Paul and I have given talks and 'trailers' at various events.

Cost

The first one was not cheap! We used a professional band and professional sound and lighting because we wanted a high-quality event. Gradually we have found skilled local musicians and good sound engineers and visual technicians. If we were to stage it again in the cathedral, the total cost would be around £2,000 for the whole evening, inclusive of bands, sound, lighting and pizzas.

Resources

We have not had to create that many new resources. It has been amazing to find a rich seam of material across various traditions – Iona, *Common Worship*, Roman Catholic resources and *The Book of Uncommon Prayer*.[6] We have used ideas from the Late Late Service, Glasgow, as well as material we have written ourselves and simple ideas from youth-work resources which have been adapted for worship.

> The key resource for good liturgy is good people. Young people from a variety of churches have been more than happy to fully take part. I think that they are happier to explore ritual, symbol and gesture because it means something to them.

The word 'liturgy' means 'work of the people' – and that's what the liturgy has been. The key resource for good liturgy is good people. Young people from a variety of churches have been more than happy to fully take part. I think that they are happier to explore ritual, symbol and gesture because it means something to them. They are not just 'doing jobs' or taking part in a sketch, but building the liturgy; and therefore they feel a part of the whole thing.

What are we learning?

We have now put on four Critical Masses in different contexts, a town church in Northampton, a small rural deanery youth service, Peterborough Cathedral and a church secondary school. We have had over 800 people in total at these services, and more are planned.

We are learning that as well as helping young people understand the Eucharist, we are providing something which is being owned by young people. This is not entertainment, or led from up front. The strength of the Eucharist is in the presidency rather than leadership. The celebrant presides over the gathering, but everyone is bringing and often creating their own offering, before receiving from God. Everyone is an active participant in the whole process. It is hard in worship such as this to stand back or observe, so everyone is drawn in to the drama.

We recognize that we are inviting people to a party with food – it is a celebration.

At the start we took too much time over each of the sections and as a result we weren't very high church but very long church. The first service lasted just under three hours. The whole experience is now two hours.

We are learning that you don't really need to do much to a straight Common Worship Eucharist service to make it vibrant and alive. We found the cathedral a wonderful home for something which was recognized as liturgical excellence.

We learnt that it is important to have a strong, focused theme and to base the whole service around it. That way, through the liturgy you end up addressing one issue or aspect of Christ from lots of different directions, thus providing entry points for almost everyone.

We are learning that quality food is important. Having a couple of pizza companies who are willing to provide decent food for 200+ hungry young people has made a huge difference and helps the young people literally leave with a taste of quality in their mouths.

We have also learnt that this is not difficult. All it takes is a few creative people who are liturgically sensitive and away you go!

Future vision for Critical Mass

In a word, franchises! One deanery wants to run a regular young Mass now based on the model we have been using, and we will be helping to set this up.

We plan to stage it as a regular Diocesan Youth Mass in the cathedral. We also hope to produce some resources, music and a simple how-to-do-it guide.

Is this mission-shaped church?

No, not yet! It could be. It is a fresh expression of worship and may well grow into a worship plant. Much more likely it is a central diocesan model which we hope will act as a catalyst and will encourage other local expressions of worship for young people.

Who is coming?

Originally, the vision for the worship had been to encourage and inspire groups of young people who perhaps felt a little isolated in their own churches faithfully ploughing away each Sunday. They have come and have enjoyed the event. What we were not expecting was the large numbers of young people who might be more familiar with a different setting such as Soul Survivor or a different worship experience. Large numbers have really connected with this and participated and have not felt threatened or lost at all.

Reflecting on this we feel this is because this is not a Roman Catholic example of youth worship, but is a fusion of many styles and traditions, from renewal to Celtic to Catholic. Drawing these elements together to create something different has meant that there are entry points for most people and also a challenge to go deeper and think more about what is going on. We are learning that while grown-ups and the Church at large might still be getting hot under the collar about liturgical differences and maintaining various traditions, most young people couldn't give a stuff. They want to be taken seriously and to participate in quality worship where they are treated with respect and where they experience God in a variety of different ways rather than being entertained.

And finally ...What about the young person carrying the 'Jesus Stick'?

No, he didn't come. But I have no doubt that many more young people are now recognizing not the stick, but the presence of Jesus in the Eucharist, and that encountering Jesus has impacted their lives and helped them feel more part of the Church.

Questions for discussion

1. Why has 24-7 found such a resonance among young people? What is it that attracts them? How can we incorporate that into other elements of youth ministry?

2. Tim describes how young people from both catholic and charismatic backgrounds are able to connect with Critical Mass. Why does it work like that? What can we learn from this example?

3. How does your church building affect your mission with and to young people, both positively and negatively? Is the church building always the best place to have a service? Think through the pros and cons.

4. What are the 'non-negotiables' in our traditions when trying to engage with young people? What can we remix and what do we need to leave alone?

5. Do we really want young people as part of our church? What impact might this have on the preferred styles of worship of both adults and young people?

Further resources

For more on the 24-7 prayer movement, see www.24-7prayer.com and

Pete Greig and Dave Roberts, *Red Moon Rising*, Kingsway, 2004.

Sacred Spaces: www.sacredspaces.ie

Youth Emmaus 2: Big issues and holy spaces (details below) contains seven creative worship sessions.

Further reading

Richard Giles, *Creating Uncommon Worship*, Canterbury, 2004.

Richard Giles, *Repitching the Tent*, Canterbury, 2004.

Dot Gosling, Sue Mayfield, Tim Sledge and Tony Washington, *Youth Emmaus 2: Big issues and holy spaces*, Church House Publishing, 2006.

Jean Kerr, 'Creative approaches to existing liturgy', in Mark Montgomery (ed.), *Young People and Worship*, Church House Publishing, 2007. *Young People and Worship* as a whole contains many useful contributions.

Part Three

Where do we go from here?
A youth-mission-shaped church

8 Overview of the case studies: challenges and encouragements for the wider Church

Chris Russell

One of my favourite episodes of the best-loved cartoon of our times, The Simpsons, starts like ths.

> The scene is the front room of the Simpsons' family home in Springfield. The front door bursts open and Bart, Lisa and Homer run in taking their clothes off, followed by a nonplussed Marge.
>
> *Lisa, Bart*: Hurray, Hurray!
>
> *Homer*: Oh man, am I glad to get out of there.
>
> *Marge*: Calm down, calm down, you're wrinkling your church clothes.
>
> *Homer*: Who cares? This is the best part of the week . . .
>
> *Lisa*: It's the longest possible time before more church!
>
> *Marge*: Church shouldn't be a chore – it should help you with your daily life.
>
> *Homer*: It should. But it doesn't. Now who'll come with me to the dump?

This scene, funny as it is, feels so poignant to those of us who are consumed with the vocation to see the Church of Jesus Christ be all it could be for this generation. Like much comedy, it plays on shared assumptions and experiences: special clothes for church, the relief of church services having finished, not looking forward to being at church, and perhaps most devastating of all is the assumption that church does not even get close to delivering what it says on the tin.

But rather than spend time in a hand-wringing critique of what's wrong, let's focus our energies on how the Church can be all it is called to be for this emerging generation.

> ❝Let's focus our energies on how the Church can be all it is called to be for this emerging generation.❞

The aim of this chapter is twofold: first, I seek to draw out from the case studies presented above particular challenges and encouragements for the wider Church. Then I'll address and clarify some of the key questions raised by the practices and reflections set out in the book.

In Chapter 9, I seek to throw down the gauntlet as to the essential nature of Church and its vocation to this postmodern generation.[1] Finally, I seek to offer a glimpse of what a youth-mission-shaped church might look like, not as a definitive one-size-fits-all model, but as a frame around which particular projects may build.

However, from the start I declare my hand. I do not come to project from a neutral stance or as an observer. For the past five years I have been vicar of St Laurence, Reading, a church whose vocation is to see unchurched young people come to faith and to build new models of church with them (www.saintlaurencereading.com). Week by week, around 50 adults and 50 teenagers gather to worship and live God's life together, with a further 200 young people locating themselves somewhere in the life of the community of the church. We have a wonderful twelfth-century building in the heart of Reading, with more opportunities than we know what to do with, and a fire in our hearts to see Reading change one young life at a time. It has been much harder than we ever thought it would be, in terms of cost, strategy, practice, hopes and fruit. But we remain more than ever excited by and committed to this particular vision.

While there are many things we are still discerning, imagining and implementing, there is one thing we are more convinced of than ever and that is the essential place of the Church in God's strategy for his world. Over the last few years I have become a lover of the Church – a defender not of an institution, but of a divine approach to living God's life, being his people and doing his work.

Refreshingly then, the book you hold in your hand doesn't start from the premise that the Church has got it all wrong in its mission to young people.

Instead it starts from the desire to do something new for God for young people, beginning with sensing what God is already doing among them and the commitment given by many up and down this country to serving in this work.

At this point it is important to acknowledge the diversity of relationships to Church represented by the case studies. While not all of the projects featured in this book would describe themselves as seeking to 'do', to 'be' or to 'build' church, there is for them all, at least some essential relationship to Church, be it with work grown organically out of a local church, or deanery or diocesan-wide initiative. For me, the fact that there is such a diversity of projects, with a pooling of resources across churches and church traditions, speaks volumes of the commitment of many to work this out in equally risky, but extraordinarily different ways. Each initiative has at its beating heart a priority of mission to young people and what I seek to explore is the relationship between mission directed towards young people and the Church. This raises questions about the definition of 'Church', explored in greater depth in the next chapter. At this point, we need simply to acknowledge that this is part of a wider debate about the nature of Church that is going on in every diocese and indeed every denomination in the country.[2]

> Each initiative has at its beating heart a priority of mission to young people.

Many discussions about 'fresh expressions'/ 'emerging church'/ 'new forms of church'[3] revolve around the use of the term 'church' itself. It seems that many initiatives claiming legitimacy under the 'new form of church' label, are actually doing things that the Church has been doing for a long time, but which are just being rebranded. A friend who is an evangelist shared his concern with me that some of the initiatives that might now refer to themselves as church, would traditionally have been seen as evangelistic strategies, projects or initiatives, and that in all the talk of mission, the essential evangelistic element of mission has been sidelined. Certainly there is a question of what church is, what it looks like, but several of the projects described here don't claim to 'be church', rather they are simply trying to engage young people with the gospel in fresh ways. What these projects demonstrate then, is a confidence in the gospel being good news to today's young people, and a tangible commitment to see that lived out.

Challenges to the wider Church

We turn now to look at some of the specific challenges arising from the case studies. The challenges below are part of a bigger prophetic challenge to the rest of the Church, and addressing them may enable the whole Church to discern its true identity more clearly.

Challenge no. 1: to be orientated to the marginalized

Anyone who has ever been involved in seeking to be part of a church that desires to grow has, surely, toyed with the idea of going to the group that might be easiest to reach, those for whom coming to faith and becoming part of the church might not be so much of a seismic shift in culture, values and practice. While the Church has often been at the forefront of working with the marginalized, evangelistic initiatives have tended to be best-resourced among educated and middle-class people. However, many people sense that actually part of the challenge of Jesus is to go to those who are most in need.

❝While the Church has often been at the forefront of working with the marginalized, evangelistic initiatives have tended to be best-resourced among educated and middle-class people. However, many people sense that actually part of the challenge of Jesus is to go to those who are most in need.❞

There are more socially excluded young people in Britain than ever before. So while it is true that there are more young people going to university and in further education, there are also more leaving school with fewer than 5 A–C grades at GCSE. There are increases in teenage levels of crime and addiction, in teenage pregnancy and sexually transmitted diseases, in unemployment and disaffection with the political process. While the social mainstream has got broader, warmer and faster, more have washed up at the margins, for whom the mainstream is unreachable. What is particularly poignant about some of the contributions of this book is that many local Christians have chosen to locate their time, resources and energies in being *for* these young people, the ones that statutory and voluntary agencies term 'hard to reach'. The Grafted project in the Scottish Borders seeks to engage those who are left out of the onwards and upwards aspirations of educated young people, and this is just one example of many projects around the country which are seeking to make life different for those whose lives are most difficult.

> ❝The challenge of working with excluded young people applies to all of us: what is it that each of us is called to do for those who are less well off?❞

The challenge to us is not to simply let ourselves off the hook because someone else is at the edges doing the work with the marginalized, nor to believe that the wider Church can fulfil the mandate to be *for* those who are most in need just by reading their information, by giving money or praying. I want to argue that the challenge of working with excluded young people applies to all of us: what is it that each of us is called to do for those who are less well off? The challenge is for all of us: in the localities we are in, where and how are we seeking to love those who are overlooked?

Challenge no. 2: to focus resources on mission

Each of the projects described in this book has been costly. Individuals and groups have given of themselves and given financially to facilitate projects that invite young people to explore, encounter, discover and be transformed by the living God and his ways. To this end, individuals and groups, diocese and deaneries have made the allocation of resources into such risky initiatives a priority. Each mission-shaped project stands as a challenge as to how churches and individual Christians use and steward resources. If mission is as much a priority as maintaining what we already have, then that will be seen in the money, energy and resources we give to it. A couple of the contributors comment that the financial cost is huge, but surely we are left

> ❝If mission is as much a priority as maintaining what we already have, then that will be seen in the money, energy and resources we give to it.❞

wondering what could be achieved if mission projects such as these were made financial priorities. It is my contention that the Church of England is uniquely placed to resource and enable mission to all of England.

Challenge no. 3: to be the Church serving the kingdom

A distinct focus on the end of seeing faith come alive in individuals and seeing them become a part of the Church, carries with it the danger that we can become preoccupied with the life of the church, as if it were an end in itself. Bishop Graham Cray is often heard to say, 'I don't care how high a view of church you have, as long as you have a higher view of the kingdom of God.' For the church should serve the kingdom, offering acts of service to the wider community with no strings attached, simply because those outside the church are still made in the image of God and therefore have an intrinsic worth. In many of the projects described in this book we see members of the church serving the kingdom of God outside the bounds of the church, in school or on estates, in gathering together young Christians to fire them up to work for God's kingdom wherever they are. The challenge for the wider Church is not simply to build church but to give ourselves sacrificially, in imaginative and costly ways, so that the boundaries of the kingdom are extended.

> The challenge for the wider Church is not simply to build church but to give ourselves sacrificially, in imaginative and costly ways, so that the boundaries of the kingdom are extended.

Challenge no. 4: to realize that mission is not the preserve of specialists or outsiders

In the mid 1980s I was involved in a mission at my local church called Youthquake. Everyone got mobilized, everyone got 'trained up', everyone got praying, but the key element was someone from outside coming in to do the 'real stuff'. Surely one of the most exciting things in the last two decades, however, has been the realization that the local church itself is actually the best tool of mission. Mission has become far less about individuals, about outsiders, about specialists coming in to 'do the stuff'. Rather, it's

> God has called, equipped and used *people like us*. There is no hanging around waiting for the expert to turn up, no application of 'off-the-shelf' strategies.

about us. There is clearly is a need to work out how the gifts of those called specifically to be evangelists can be used for the sake of the wider Church. But what is clear from what we have read in this book, is that God has called, equipped and used *people like us*. There is no hanging around waiting for the expert to turn up, no application of 'off-the-shelf' strategies. Rather, God's essential work of reaching out is effective through individuals and groups hearing the call and being willing to take a risk.

The prophetic challenges described above are not only arising in work with young people, but it does seem that when we reflect on the challenges and opportunities of working with young people we see a microcosm of what is true of the Church's work with the wider society.

It is worth reflecting also on the shift of attitude and approach of Christians to working with young people revealed by much of what we have read. Some important issues are raised, which help us to articulate why Church matters and what it needs to be, questions of primary importance to mission with this next generation.

Most of the significant work with young people in the last century was carried out apart from the local church. So any history of work with young people would need to talk of work in universities by UCCF and SCM, work in evangelism by groups such as Youth For Christ and YWAM, the annual events which have shaped and defined young people's spirituality and engagement such as Greenbelt, Spring Harvest and Soul Survivor.[4] Then there is the agenda setting and resourcing of Oasis, 24-7 and other organizations harnessing the passion of young people to work for a better world, such as Tearfund, Christian Aid and World Vision. The present state of the Church owes much to these parachurch organizations.[5] Yet very few of them directly addressed the state of the Church. A friend of mine complained while we were returning from a conference run by one of the groups,

> It's always wonderful to sense God working in you so personally. But when I come back from these intense times away, I feel that God has given me a whole new load of software. And I go to my church and all they have to play it on is some clapped out Amstrad or ZX81.

That is, the focus rarely addressed the corporate life of faith in a local setting, other than being told to 'stick at it'.

Today the sense is that this is not a time for new parachurch organizations, but for energy to be given to working out what it is local church needs to be, especially if young people are going to be valued as essential members of the church. There seem, then, essential elements we need to take with utter seriousness if we are going to address the kind of church we need to be for unchurched young people.

Issues for a youth-mission-shaped Church

So what are the core issues that a youth-mission-shaped Church will be aware of and dealing with?

Culture

If we focus for a moment on individual churches, we become aware of the ever-widening chasm between the culture of the church and the culture of young people. It was said over two decades ago that for an adult to become a member of the Church, there were two conversions necessary, one to Christ and one to the culture of the Church. Imagine how much harder it is for a contemporary adult or young person. As Graham Cray pointed out in Chapter 2, most unchurched young people today have virtually no understanding of the central beliefs of Christianity. Indeed, it is commonplace for young people to express opinions that Jesus is as mythical as Father Christmas, or to admit that they have never opened a Bible outside an RE lesson or stepped inside a church building by personal choice. This doesn't necessarily mean that young people are anti-Christian, but it does mean that nothing can be taken for granted of the knowledge they do, or do not, bring with them.

Not only is that so, but to imagine that unchurched young people are in some neutral ground, blank sheets of paper awaiting tools to enable them to make sense of life, is ill-founded. When my daughter was three we were together in the kitchen and I picked her up to put her on the work surface.

'Be careful with me, Daddy,' she said. Fascinating, I thought.

'Why should I be careful Hopey?' I asked.

'Because I'm precious,' she said.

'Why are you precious?'

'Because God made me and loves me.'

This little interchange with my contrary daughter hit me between the eyes. My wife and I are seeking to bring our children up to know their worth in God's eyes, to believe that God not only made them but loves them, that they needn't be afraid at night because he is with them, that when they fall and hurt themselves we can pray that God would heal them. We hope and pray they will grow up in this reality and find it to be true.

> When I say to Saskia that she is worth more than she can ever imagine because she is made in the image of God, this is news to her. There is no way she can grasp what it means or even trust it quickly.

Yet the teenagers I live among have no such awareness. When I say to Saskia that she is worth more than she can ever imagine because she is made in the image of God, this is news to her. There is no way she can grasp what it means or even trust it quickly. The Christian faith is giving these young people a totally new way of seeing themselves and the world, to say nothing of utterly redefining one of the most misunderstood words of our culture, 'God'. Young people do not start in some neutral territory, at 0, but at minus-70. The effect of breathing the air of a consumerist, idolatrous culture, where beauty, pleasure, self, fame and acquiring 'stuff' are all worshipped, has a drastic effect on young people.

On top of this our young people are used to a different way of constructing reality, defining meaning, showing value and expression themselves. This can be seen in attitudes towards bodies – in piercings, tattoos, self-harm, in approaches to sex and sexuality. Major issues of a generation ago are no longer issues. These days, if you were to try giving a classic Christian talk from 20 years ago on sex or 'how far you should go' to any group but the most sheltered of Christian young people, you would find yourself in an utterly different landscape. On top of this there is the general antipathy towards institutions and their representatives. The lack of trust in people who aren't peers and the shrug of the shoulders attitude towards Christianity as an organized religion is so prevalent as to make one wonder if it's something in the ketchup. If this is true even in some cases, how does the Church go about engaging with those who do not even acknowledge our presence as positive?

Spirituality

While in the 1980s and 1990s it was commonplace to hear people make excited connections between what we were told was the rise in interest in spirituality and opportunities to introduce the Christian faith, some recent studies of young people's approach to spirituality have questioned whether what is widely accepted as spiritual practice offers any obvious leads to Christian practice. In *Making Sense of Generation Y* [6] the authors present findings from their research interviews with young people aged 15 to 25, interviews in which any connections between the young people's spirituality and the Christian faith were explored. The authors found that most young people express a sense of 'formative spirituality', that is, an inherent, implicit sense and practice which expresses itself in ways regarded as mainstream culturally – flowers at scenes of accidents, interest and passive involvement in beliefs and customs which nod to something other than the material – but with no expectation or hope that life in the here and now might be affected. So while formative spirituality might be seen in general discourse, in superstition, in attitudes, expressions, experiences and practices, this has little or no consequence to the individual concerned. What is more, there is no direct link between such formative spirituality and what they term a 'transformative spirituality', which involves the individual in deliberate practices – prayer, meditation, particular beliefs and faith communities – which one chooses to involve oneself in because of the hope that they will change both the person and the present situation. Such practices have an obvious and tangible value in the lives of those who practise them.

We do not have space here to explore the fascinating findings of this study, yet it is pertinent to question the 'inherent connection' and 'obvious opportunity' many in the Church have suggested between popular spiritual expression and Christian faith. It is my contention that while young people's attitude to spirituality may sometimes offer an openness to taking part in Christian spiritual practices, it in no way is a straight line which takes a young person from the spiritual mindset of an unchurched teenager to Christian prayer, worship or encounter with God.

For these young people there has never been a conscious decision not to go to church, not to investigate the truth of the claims of this Jesus of Nazareth. On the whole it would never occur to them to contemplate even investigating them. These attitudes are taken as read. One thing this does mean is that some young people will call themselves Christian if they have chosen to step into that for themselves.

What's more, it is surely questionable for the Church to seek to reach the younger generation by offering the answer to questions that few are asking. For example, the tag line in an advertisement trying to interest people in an evangelistic initiative has the usual line-up of the successful, famous and beautiful people saying 'There must be more to life than this?' But very few people in this generation wrestle with this question. It feels to me as if by marketing the gospel round such questions, we show how we have misread our culture and not really listened. As much as it might disappoint us and amaze us, the young people I know who regularly take drugs, drink, live chaotic and shambolic lives, are unable to hold down steady relationships, don't spend their first hour in bed at night wishing they could find some meaning in life. There just doesn't seem to be a huge yearning for 'more than this'. That simply is not the issue.

In the first place, theologically it falls into the trap Bonhoeffer noted, of speaking of a God of the gaps, where God is reduced to a means to explain what normal life can't. Bonhoeffer's great desire was to speak of God 'at the centre of life'. Yes, there might be more to life than this, even for a beautiful model, climber, footballer – but for this generation it is with the very stuff of this life that Christian faith needs to intersect. It is in the day-to-day round of relationships, work, school, family, habits, excess, desires, compulsions, money and health that the gospel has its obvious and most transformative connections. The more we restrict faith to supplying answers to what lies beyond daily life, the existential questions and the spiritual practices, the less surprised we should be that few want to know.

> For this generation it is with the very stuff of this life that Christian faith needs to intersect. It is in the day-to-day round of relationships, work, school, family, habits, excess, desires, compulsions, money and health that the gospel has its obvious and most transformative connections.

With a culture built around an exhausting rate of change, access to technology and information, the exposure to prevailing trends and habits, set against a fairly defined, permanent church culture, it sometimes can feel that the culture of church and the culture of young people widens by the month. What then of the culture of the church which takes seriously its mission to those who are in this generation?

Christian culture

This situation is not really solved by the Christian youth culture. For those of us who take unchurched young people to national Christian youth events the contrast between the two cultures is starkly defined. What is the task to which we must address ourselves? Is our primary task to be *relevant*? My perspective is that to put relevance first is to let the tail wag the dog. Rather, our primary task is to be *authentic*. To seek to allow a young person to be authentically a young person and authentically a Christian is the charge. The challenge for the Church is not primarily to set up culturally relevant forms of church, but to allow young people to be authentically themselves, part of this generation, and to be authentically Christian. But what are the essential elements for this, and who decides?

9 What might a youth-mission-shaped church look like?

Chris Russell

In this chapter we will first of all look at the essential elements of Church – what it is and why it matters. We will then go on to outline three 'pivots' around which a youth-mission-shaped church might develop and grow.

Church: what it is and why it matters

While it is by no means the case that all the examples in the book are addressing directly the nature and form of church, it could be said that each of them begs questions of what 'church' actually is. The gatherings of local young people in central venues, the work in schools, the occasional town-wide gathering –they don't claim to be church explicitly, but should they? And if not, what is their relationship to church? Encouragingly, much of what we have read doesn't start from the negative position of what isn't right, with what isn't going on, but with what God is doing. Far from the Church being apart from this, The Church is essential to the initiation, delivery and fulfilment of mission in this emerging generation.

> The Church is essential to the initiation, delivery and fulfilment of mission in this emerging generation.

As has been said above, one of the things that the whole mission-shaped church discourse has brought about is a need for some deep thought as to what we actually mean by 'church'. Many of us who are involved in what might be termed 'fresh expressions of church' feel that our ecclesiology is far less developed than it should be. That may be a fault of those on whose shoulders we stand, as well as our own fault. However, what are those essential things we want to stand as non-negotiable, which define 'church'?

Church is ... rooted in God

There are of course as many definitions of 'church' as there are projects, but what is key for us all is the reminder that this church is not some humanly ordained, volitional community. Rather, church is a community of people who owe all to the person and work of the triune God revealed in Jesus of Nazareth. Deep in the fabric of our being, we are Trinitarian. We do not gather ourselves together and then embark on the task of relating to this triune God in worship, service or witness. Rather, the Spirit so works in us that we respond to the love of the Father in the person of Christ, that he bonds us to him, and together in Christ by the power of the Spirit we are defined by him. As church we are called to try to live in appropriate response to the reality of God. It is because of this God that we are, that we are together, and that we are together for this world.

Church, therefore, is God-given and our being, form and *raison d'etre* reflect his.[1] At the very least then, this gives significance to the essentially corporate nature of church against institutional hierarchy, the relational power of the church's life, and to the legitimacy of love, acceptance, hospitality and sacrifice as the currency of the church's mission.

Church is ... called for the sake of others

In Scripture, election (that is, God's choice of a particular person, family or nation) has a particular end: others. The end of God's calling is never the one called, he calls a particular person, family or nation for the sake of others – those who are called are sent. From Genesis 12 throughout the Old Testament the people of God are called to be a blessing to others. The tragedy seems to be, then, that this election is seen by God's people in the Old Testament as something of a badge of ownership, rather than a vocation. God's people were called to be a light to the Gentiles. Their failing was in omitting to live this out. Jesus of Nazareth is the one who comes to fulfil what they did not, *he* is the light to the Gentiles, the chosen one for the sake of others, the one in whom God is uniquely present, choosing to act for the sake of the blessing of the world.

The nature, form and vocation of the Church of Jesus Christ are *ipso facto* defined by the nature, form and vocation of the life of Christ. So the Church exists for God, and because of who this God is and how he is, because of what he has done and wills to do, the *raison d'etre* is found in the person of Christ. Christ both lived to the glory of the Father in the power of the Spirit, and was the 'man for others'. Therefore just as Luther defined sin as a heart curved in on itself, the definition of a sinful church is a church curved in on itself, one that is concerned primarily with its own life.[2] In such a church the main objective is 'me' expressing 'my' faith, having my needs met, and our meetings being a place where people like me attempt to do all this without getting bored. No, the agenda is not mine, not yours, not even primarily those who aren't in church yet, but God's. And being orientated around God invites, no, stronger than that, *demands*, being orientated around those he loves, those whom he travelled into the far-off country to bring home.

> Just as Luther defined sin as a heart curved in on itself, the definition of a sinful church is a church curved in on itself, one that is concerned primarily with its own life.

The Church, therefore, is for others, and particularly, in Bonhoeffer's words, for those yet to come. Faced with the hardest decision of his life, whether to hold to his personal ethics, or take a course of action he felt deeply uneasy about for the sake of his country, Bonhoeffer chose the latter, and so joined the bomb plot to kill Hitler. Of this he wrote: 'The ultimate question for a responsible man to ask is not how he is to extricate himself heroically . . . but how the coming generation is to live.'[3]

> A church that exists for others must constantly ask, 'How then will the next generation live?'

A church that exists for others must constantly ask, 'How then will the next generation live?' And for this generation of young people old distinctions and reservations about the relationship between justice and proclamation, between doing the works of the kingdom and introducing the king, are lost.

The Church is ... a response to and vessel for the gospel

Lastly, the church will seek to be an adequate vessel for the gospel. The church is a response to the gospel, seeking to live in thanks for all that has taken hold of us.

'The activity of the community is related to the Gospel only in so far as it is no more than a crater formed by the explosion of a shell.'[4] The church's task is to be alive by and for the one who died and rose again for it, and to witness to this one who raises the dead. This is the God who is constantly doing new things, always in line with who he has revealed himself to be in Christ, but as Walter Brueggemann says, 'God isn't a word for what is already happening.'[5] The church bears witness to the good news of the transformative work of God for us in Christ, in words, action, testimony and experience.

The Church of Jesus Christ is a 'come and see' community, where what is proclaimed is truly known and experienced as real, where the one whose name we bear is encountered and tasted in the life of his people.

> ❝The Church of Jesus Christ is a 'come and see' community, where what is proclaimed is truly known and experienced as real, where the one whose name we bear is encountered and tasted in the life of his people.❞

In all this it is my contention that the Church of Jesus Christ is God's uniquely appointed vehicle to bear witness to his life and present reality and to continue his work. And if that is anywhere near close to stating God's intention for this body, defining the make-up, and probing the essential elements of what we need to do and be, are essential for any community seeking to be authentically church. Historical definitions must be weighed and taken on, for example the place of the sacraments of baptism and the Eucharist, the proclamation of the word, the centrality of worship, of oversight, permission and resourcing, will need addressing. How is the church that seeks to be for this generation consistent with the one, holy, catholic and apostolic church? This is not the place, nor have we the space to do these questions justice, but it is certainly required that we weigh the inheritance for which we are deeply thankful, and that we rise to the challenge to stand responsibly in that tradition, while daring to reimagine who God's people must be for such a time as this.

But if being rooted in God, being for others, and seeking to be a response to the gospel are taken as essential determinants for the Church, what then is the shape this life takes in a youth-mission-shaped church?

The shape of a youth-mission-shaped church

At this point I have to confess to a certain reticence to set out anything concrete. While I believe strongly in the catholicity of the Church, it seems to me that in each locality the people of God have to discern for themselves what shape God's life in and through them should take. Paramount to this will be the particular context of each community, and those they are called to serve. One of the things that is surely so puzzling is how so many church plants in the past decades have not really taken account of the locality in which they have been sown, nor whom they are called to serve. Vast resources have been made available for what I call Franchise Church Plants. Franchise outlets occur throughout our towns and cities. Whenever KFC or MacDonalds arrive in a new place, they set up shop in exactly the way they have done it everywhere else. There is no variation, and the only concession to the area is payment in the local currency. They use the same uniforms, the same way of cooking chips, the same menu, the same brand. Too many church plants seem to have done the same.

The time for Franchise Church Plants is over (if it ever existed at all). The task of new forms of church is to be an appropriate echo of the life of God, to incarnate his life in this particular setting for these particular people. I offer three essential pivots around which such life grows.

Pivot no. 1: worship

If God is the one whom any church serves, reflects and is determined by worship will be at the heart of the life of the people of God. Indeed there is something essentially given about the priority of attending to God. The church's main responsibility is to seek to attend to God – who he is and how he is, and that this is almost so obvious as to be taken as read, but is passed over and taken for granted at our peril. Eugene Peterson constantly makes the point that one of the prime callings of the Church is to give people the words, actions, senses and ability to respond to God.[6] He argues that human beings are tool-making creatures; we use knives and forks to eat, spades to dig, pens to write, words to communicate. So with our life with God, we need tools. Churches are the workshops of prayers, songs and public worship which are exactly about giving humans tools with which to connect with God, truly and authentically.

> ❝The church's main responsibility is to seek to attend to God – who he is and how he is, and that this is almost so obvious as to be taken as read, but is passed over and taken for granted at our peril.❞

This means that a vital task of a youth-mission-shaped church is to offer habitable and hospitable patterns and ways of worshipping which are authentic to Christianity and to the culture of the young people who comprise the church. Particularly helpful in this is the distinction between form and content.

> ❝A vital task of a youth-mission-shaped church is to offer habitable and hospitable patterns and ways of worshipping which are authentic to Christianity and to the culture of the young people who comprise the church.❞

It seems relatively clear that Christians have always done specific things when they have gathered together, involving praise, prayer, word, sacrament and confession. We take these then as the constituent elements, the content of church praxis and identity, the bare bones of the content of Christian worship. These things are not up for grabs. We do not meet and simply exchange opinions about what we should or could do, what we feel like doing, what we think might work. We attend to God in ways that are historically consistent. Authentic and orthodox Christian worship has certain non-negotiable elements. But how those elements and how that content is expressed differs depending on the context of those who gather. The fact that often the form which this content takes is so alien to the culture of young people seems to enable attitudes towards church which see it as entirely immaterial to the rest of life. And Christian worship then inoculates young people against responding to the gospel and truly engaging with God.

It seems clear that while the content has remained constant, the form has constantly evolved, depending on the particular situation and conditions. What congregations can feel threatened by is a change in form, as they can easily feel that the content is being challenged or removed. This rarely is the case, and it is of the utmost importance that the two are separated. The vocation of a church seeking to be *for* young people is to practise the authentic content of Christian worship in a form which is authentic to those who gather. This will mean profound questions and issues for worship, for the proclamation of the word, for sacramental practice and for prayer. Some of these things will be deeply countercultural and will need wise explaining and accounting for. For example, it will be deeply puzzling for many young people to see priority being given to gathering around Scripture, to sung praise, to prayer for the world. That these don't fit with the culture isn't a good enough reason to ditch them. But it is my contention that there has not been enough engagement with creative imagination in what form this content might take.

In Susan Howatch's novel *Glamorous Powers* the priest John Darrowby is trying to explain to his grown-up, non-churchgoing daughter the purpose of liturgy.[7] He says that liturgy is like the lines on a page that enable you to write straight. This I am sure was true for a particular generation. But for a church which seeks to be for young people who have had no previous contact with church, it feels often as if the participants are not even used to writing on lines, they are more used to drawing pictures or sketching diagrams. So what should the liturgy of worship look like for this generation, when the inherited models are culturally bound to a very literate, modernistic mindset?

Pivot no. 2: belonging

When I met my wife I was serving my title in a small parish in southeast London. She was a member of a house church on the south coast. During the heady weeks of introducing ourselves and finding out about each other I expressed a strong desire to 'come and see her church'. She replied that the worst thing for me to do was to visit on a Sunday, because often the meetings were fairly chaotic and hit-and-miss. No, she said, if you want to know what my church is like come down and live in Chichester for a week, see how people welcome you, see what they do with their time, their money, their houses, their relationships. Come and live with people, then you will get an idea of what the church is like. I was amazed. I remember thinking, 'imagine having that much confidence in your church'.

I wonder whether sometimes so much effort is put into Sunday services because there is nothing else behind them. We have reduced the life of the church to how well things go in an hour or two on Sunday. And while, of course, our corporate worship is an essential determinant for our life together, we are not reducible to it. Our corporate worship is, then, an expression of who we are before the face of God. It is not a moment out of time, but a moment which is reflective of the life of the body.

Any youth-mission-shaped church will be at the heart of things a community of people. Young people will, surprisingly quickly, use terms such as family, safety, acceptance, love, friendship, and sense that they matter. Community life isn't a means to get them to the end of life with God. This is the thing itself. This is the life of God lived in the corporate body.

> ❝Any youth-mission-shaped church will be at the heart of things a community of people. Young people will, surprisingly quickly, use terms such as family, safety, acceptance, love, friendship, and sense that they matter.❞

There is then among many of the emerging generation who are involved in these adventures of faith an air of bafflement that church for so long didn't mean belonging, community and corporate identity. An individualistic age loves the poem of a man looking at his life as a set of footprints along a beach, and seeing only one set of footprints carrying him in the hard times of his life. This generation see the multitude of footprints carrying them in the hard times of their lives, because Christ carries through his church. And church is essentially about belonging to a community of people.

This means that there is an 'of course' to much that has been offered in the mission-shaped church discourse when it talks of community. The community of faith will be diverse and broad, including those who would not themselves say they were on the journey of faith. So at St Laurence there are around

> **❝**There are those who are on the edge of the confessional life of the church who flow in and out depending on other circumstances in their lives. But the sense of corporate belonging holds everyone in.**❞**

200 young people who would say they were part of the church, but there are concentric circles of involvement and of commitment to each other and to Christ. Those on the outside circle still count themselves as part of the church, but they do not yet come to anything we do confessionally. There are those who are on the edge of the confessional life of the church who flow in and out depending on other circumstances in their lives. But the sense of corporate belonging holds everyone in.

Relationships are what it is all about – relationships with God, with each other, with those who are not like us. A community is able to incarnate the life of Christ in a locality precisely because it is a community. I am entirely perplexed by where the populist notion that 'Christian' means 'little Christ' comes from. Rather, the gospel seems to save me from the notion that I am the messiah. On my own I am not the hands of Christ, the ears of Christ, the mouth of Christ. As an individual I do not have to be Jesus to people. Jesus Christ is alive and fully able to do that himself. But corporately, as part of this body as we all play our essential parts, we are *together* the hands of Christ, the heart of Christ, the life of Christ to and for those we are called to.

For this to be reality, our experience is that all ages and backgrounds are valuable. The aim is not to build hybrid or exclusive churches around certain age groups. A church may have a distinctive missiological focus – normally this is the locality of the parish, but for some of us it is an age group. But in order to really see the community of faith established, I wonder whether there needs to be a non-age-specific church which has an age-specific mission. So perhaps there needs to be less talk of youth churches, and more talk of churches where anyone God calls is welcome, but all are committed

> **❝**Perhaps there needs to be less talk of youth churches, and more talk of churches where anyone God calls is welcome, but all are committed to serving this particular age group.**❞**

to serving this particular age group. There may be different expressions of the life of the community in different congregations. It is sheer folly to think that the cultural differences represented in such a community today could be met week by week in a one-size-fits-all way. So, one church with different congregations. This has long been a regular feature of a Church of England church with an 8 o'clock *Book of Common Prayer* service, a 10.30 Family Service and a 6.30 evensong. Behind the different ways of expressing the same faith, the congregation members belong to this particular community.

Obviously this raises many questions about how this is worked out, about the characteristics of the Christian community, about how members would locate themselves in it, about the expectations that are on people in different levels of relational involvement, and who sets those and implements those. This leads us to the next pivot.

Pivot no. 3: discipleship

There are those, and they do seem to locate themselves especially in the alt worship, emerging church discourses, who seem to think that the church's obsession with discipleship has been the cause of many people leaving church. The impression they give is that because certain ways of behaving have been prescribed, many people have left. While this may be true, it always seems to give those who leave the benefit of the doubt. But the casualty in it all seems to be holiness, hard choices in behaviour and relationships, in money, possessions, where you choose to live, the job you do. For any people of God seeking to be mission-shaped among young people, discipleship will be the prime issue.

> For any people of God seeking to be mission-shaped among young people, discipleship will be the prime issue.

Previously we have referred to the research reported in *Making Sense of Generation Y*, which distinguished between formative spirituality and transformative spirituality. Practice of formative spirituality clearly does not have a direct correlation to interest in and commitment to transformative spirituality. Without a commitment to discipleship our church communities could easily become, literally, service providers, offering a place for people to engage in spiritual practices which have no consequences for their day-to-day lives.

> ❝The followers of Jesus Christ are called to *make disciples*, not just offer easy-prayer to ambient dance music.❞

It is relatively easy to provide rituals, practices and exercises for young people to engage with God. Many times these are done extraordinarily creatively and very profoundly. However, The followers of Jesus Christ are called to *make disciples*, not just offer easy-prayer to ambient dance music. This means an essential commitment to discipleship.

This cannot be done just through pre-set courses, or step-by-step easy formulas. In fact there is probably not an utterly clear view of what it is we are after, apart from a life on fire for God. Bishop Graham Cray's comments are of profound importance. He states that while it might be easy for him to think he knows what the main issues are for his teenage daughters, and how they should negotiate themselves through the perils of life, he needs to remember that some of the resources, which he could so eagerly want to give to them, are about as much use as Saul's armour was to David when he went out to fight Goliath.[8] In fact an essential part of supporting teenagers is to trust the Holy Spirit to enable them to live their lives fully for God.

A decade or so ago at any conference on the challenge the Church faced in reaching unchurched people, one dictum was wheeled out with disturbing regularity: 'behave, believe, belong', had now morphed into a general rule of 'belong, believe, behave'. So the accepted given now is that someone first needs to belong, then their behaviour will start to get in line with their faith. It was always clear this isn't an instantaneous thing, that coming to faith is a process and belonging to a group of people is probably essential to any commitment lasting. This almost doesn't seem worth stating – except for this caveat: nobody expressed how much it hurt. St Paul writes in Galatians, 'I am again in the pains of childbirth until Christ is formed in you' (Galatians 4.19). Anyone who has worked to see young people take steps in discipleship will know the joy and the agony of the ground taken and the ground lost.

However, it is either about a community of disciples seeking to follow Jesus in their everyday life, or it is nothing. Last century Bonhoeffer railed against those who allowed God to be pushed to the edges of life, to the gaps. What was needed was not some apologist argument for those things that couldn't be explained but by God. What was needed was to talk of God at the centre of life. Discipleship takes seriously the whole of a young person's

> ❝To follow this Jesus will have implications for young people's sex lives, their addictions, their families, their revenge, their criminality, their responsibility.❞

life orientated towards God, with no talk of a god of the gaps; rather this is the God of life. To follow this Jesus will have implications for young people's sex lives, their addictions, their families, their revenge, their criminality, their responsibility.

Interestingly, it is in an accepting and honest place to talk about the issues of life that many unchurched young people get engaged with the gospel. The 'How then should we live?' question is the million-dollar question for today. A gospel presented not as a list of dos and don'ts, not as an ethical code, but as a shape of living, is immensely attractive to young people. So,

> ❝The 'How then should we live?' question is the million-dollar question for today. A gospel presented not as a list of dos and don'ts, not as an ethical code, but as a shape of living, is immensely attractive to young people.❞

for example, Rachel Gardner's development of the Romance Academy is a profound way of handling a behavioural issue intrinsic to youth culture today, in a Christian way with powerful results.[9]

Following Jesus is not merely a matter of the issues preoccupying the lives of young people, but involves following him in being for others. In a self-obsessed culture which enshrines the personal tastes and fulfilment of the individual, a youth-mission-shaped church will be marked out by being orientated around the lives of others. In the DNA of the community there needs to be an orientation to others, and not just to those who are already part of the community. This means that everyone who is part of the community needs to be aware that they are not just there for themselves but for the sake of others. Service is an essential part of the kingdom. And while apparently it is surprising to many who wash their hands of this emerging generation, there is nothing that young people want to be involved in more than helping others. For the past two years we at St Laurence have run projects to Africa and Europe, working to build a community centre in rural Malawi and working in two state orphanages in Bulgaria. Every young person we took expressed more excitement, more joy and more fulfilment at being involved in these projects than in anything they had yet done in their lives. Young people don't want discipleship that doesn't cost, that doesn't practically help, that simply rearranges the internal moral furniture. It is my opinion that this generation will do more to serve God in serving the poorest, weakest, most exploited than any other.

This work with young people is no fleeting experiment. It is no trendy new thing. It is no heroic bandwagon. It is simply trying to live out some of the deepest longings expressed in Scripture.

> O God, from my youth you have taught me,
>   and I still proclaim your wondrous deeds.
> So even to old age and grey hairs,
>   O God, do not forsake me,
> until I proclaim your might
>   to all the generations to come. (Psalm 71.17, 18)

> We will tell to the coming generation
> the glorious deeds of the Lord, and his might,
>   and the wonders that he has done. (Psalm 78.4)

> One generation shall laud your works to another
>   and shall declare your mighty acts. (Psalm 145.4)

It is the contention and conviction of many of us that we are privileged to play a small part in God's redeeming work for which he has placed his Church at the centre of his world. This world, this culture. We will not get bored, we will not lose hope. The stakes could not be higher and our resolve could not be stronger. To be frank, it's not about fresh expressions of church. It's about proper church.

Postscript: What's emerging?

Tim Sudworth

In the Scripture Union resource *Christian Life and the Bible*, Conrad Gempf asks the question 'What kind of Christian are you? – Batman or Spiderman?' Now, behind the seemingly insane questions lies a serious challenge (indulge my love of comic book heroes for a few minutes and let me explain).

Bruce Wayne (aka Batman) witnessed the murder of his parents as a child. When he grew up he committed his life, and endless wealth, to fighting crime in his home city of Gotham. As he fights crime and seeks justice he uses an endless array of nifty gadgets and toys: the Batmobile, the Batcopter and the ever-present Batbelt among them. On this belt Batman has all sorts of equipment that might help him to be relevant and useful in any situation – Bat rope, Bat telescope, and so on.

Peter Parker (aka Spiderman) is a different kind of superhero. As a young teenager he found himself being bitten by a radioactive spider (I know . . . happens to me all the time . . .). Over a period of time the radioactive venom in his body began to rewrite his DNA. As a result he finds he has increased strength and can do some amazing things, such as climbing walls and firing webs from his wrists. So as he fights crime in New York Spiderman is relevant to each situation because of who he has become, and he doesn't need toys to help him fight crime.

So the question stands: are we Batman or Spiderman Christians? Do we continually look for the 'right thing to do' or the 'next big thing'? Or do we allow God to transform us and, by what we become, engage in God's mission to the world?

> The same questions can equally be applied to our churches or our youth ministries. Are we looking to do the next big thing? Or are we looking, as a Church, to be transformed by God and engage in his mission and with young people?

The same questions can equally be applied to our churches or our youth ministries. Are we looking to do the next big thing? Or are we looking, as a Church, to be transformed by God and engage in his mission and with young people?

We so easily get caught up in exciting stories and accounts of projects and ministries that have transformed lives, communities and beyond, that we sometimes fail to consider the thought that maybe God is seeking to tell us something and we are too busy doing 'the next thing' to listen to him. Seek God first, then look at what you might do as a response to that call – not the other way round.

Although the number of young people who go to any type of church is still very low, personally I am quite excited at the things that are happening around the UK in churches with young people. I hesitate to suggest we have turned any corners, and we do have more questions to be answered and battles to be fought. As Margaret Withers says in *Mission-shaped Children*, 'It is about changing the hearts and minds of adult Christians so that they can share responsibility for the Church's mission among the youngest and most vulnerable generation.'[1]

Dare I say that hundreds of churches, on a weekly basis, are sacrificially giving time and sometimes money for the sake of God's kingdom among young people? Sadly, many parishes, both urban and rural, have not the resources and capacity to instigate such work themselves. It seems a sad irony that the areas where this is truest are probably where most of the young people are found. If we do want to continue to 'turn the corner' with our work with young people, we have to address this on a national level and seek a vision and resources to do this work, learning from the projects in this book and others. If we can do this, the Church of England has a healthy future.

Notes

Introduction

1. *Mission-shaped Church*, GS 1523, Church House Publishing, 2004.
2. Presidential address to the General Synod, July 2003. See www. archbishopofcanterbury.org/sermonsandspeeches/2003.
3. Bishop Graham Cray, see the 2004 Report at www.cofe.anglican.org/about/ gensynod/proceedings/.
4. See www.freshexpressions.org.uk/section.asp?id=25.
5. Fresh Expressions, *Prospectus: Phase 2*, May 2006, p. 3.
6. Pete Ward, *Youthwork and the Mission of God*, SPCK, 1997, p. 3.

Chapter I   How did we get here? A short history of youth work

1. Danny Brierley, *Joined Up: An introduction to youth work and ministry*, Authentic Lifestyle, 2004.
2. T. W. Lacquer, *Religion and Respectability: Sunday schools and working class culture*, Yale University Press, 1976, p. 44.
3. Pete Ward, *Growing Up Evangelical*, SPCK, 1996, p. 24.
4. Brierley, *Joined Up*, p. 22.
5. Ward, *Growing Up Evangelical*, and Brierley, *Joined Up*.
6. Brierley, *Joined Up*, p. 51.

Chapter 2   The seven mission-shaped values of youth ministry

1. *Youth A Part* National Society/Church House Publishing, 1996.
2. I have developed this analysis at greater length in *Postmodern Culture and Youth Discipleship* (Grove, 1998) and in Sara Savage, Sylvia Collins-Mayo, Bob Mayo with Graham Cray, *Making Sense of Generation Y* (Church House Publishing, 2006).
3. A. Furlong and F. Cartmel, *Young People and Social Change*, Open University, 1997. Douglas Rushkof, *Children of Chaos*, HarperCollins, 1999, p. 3.
4. For recent academic analysis of youth cultures, see Steven Miles, *Youth Lifestyles in a Changing World*, Open University, 2000, and Rupa Huq, *Beyond Subculture: Pop, youth and identity in a postcolonial world*, Routledge, 2006.
5. Bob Jackson, *Hope for the Church*, Church House Publishing, 2002, p. 32.
6. E.g., the Covenanters' merger with British Youth for Christ in the late 1990s.
7. See Stuart Murray, *Post-Christendom: Church and mission in a strange new world*, Paternoster, 2004.
8. See *Making Sense of Generation Y*, e.g. p. 123. See index for further references.
9. See Leslie Francis and Mandy Robbins, *Urban Hope and Spiritual Health: The adolescent voice*, Epworth, 2005, p. 52.

10. *Youth A Part*, National Society/Church House Publishing, 1996, ch. 2.
11. Pete Ward, *Youthwork and the Mission of God*, SPCK, 1997, pp. 25–6.
12. Eddie Gibbs, *Leadership Next*, IVP, 2005, p. 32.
13. Ward, *Youthwork and the Mission of God*, ch. 3.
14. *Youth A Part*, p. 25.
15. In one sense this is not surprising as I was actively involved in drafting these sections of both documents. However, I did not consciously draw on *Youth A Part* when drafting parts of *Mission-shaped Church* (GS1523, Church House Publishing, 2004).
16. Mike Breen, *Outside In*, Scripture Union, 1993, p. 33. Mike's work at Romsey Mill, Cambridge laid the foundations for his later work with young adults at St Thomas Crookes, Sheffield. Another case of youth ministry leading the way for the adult church.
17. E.g., Bob Mayo in Savage, Mayo-Collins, Mayo with Cray, *Making Sense of Generation Y*, p. 131.
18. Helmut Thielicke, *Leadership*, vol. 9. no. 3.
19. See Savage, Mayo-Collins, Mayo with Cray, *Making Sense of Generation Y*, ch. 8 and p. 156.
20. For the story of 24-7 see Pete Greig and Dave Roberts, *Red Moon Rising*, Kingsway, 2004.
21. 'Words, works and wonders' (based on Romans 15.18,19) was the title of a conference for young leaders run for many years by Soul Survivor, Youth for Christ and Tearfund.
22. See Joyce Wills (ed.), *The Urban Adventure: Stories from Soul Survivor The Message 2000*, Soul Survivor, 2001; also *Soul in the City: Urban legends*, Soul Survivor, 2005.
23. See Matt Wilson, *Eden: Called to the streets*, Survivor, 2005; George Lings, *Encounters on the Edge No. 14: The Eden Puzzle*.
24. See L. West and P. Hopkins, *The D Factor*, Monarch, 2002.
25. Pete Ward, *Mass Culture*, Bible Reading Fellowship, 1999, p. 26.
26. See Pete Ward, *Growing Up Evangelical*, SPCK, 1996.
27. Graham Cray, *Youth Congregations and the Emerging Church*, Grove Evangelism Series 57.
28. Y Youth congregation in Whitstable. See their entry on the Fresh Expressions web site.
29. Robert Warren and Bob Jackson, *There is an Answer*, Springboard Resource Paper 1.
30. See *Making Sense of Generation Y*.
31. www.freshexpressions.org.uk.
32. For case studies on two different projects see George Lings, *Encounters on the Edge No. 4: Eternity – the beginning* and *No. 21 Reading: the signs*.
33. www.centreforyouthministry.ac.uk.
34. www.amaze.org.uk.
35. *Mission-shaped Church*, pp. 36–41.

Chapter 3   The ever-changing context of young people

1. For the most recently published figures, see www.cofe.anglican.org/info/statistics/
   churchstats2004/statisticsfront.html. The foreword to the report gives a summary of
   the findings. www.cofe.anglican.org/info/statistics/churchstats2004/foreword.html.
2. Martin Lindstrom and Patricia B. Seybold, *Brandchild*, Kogan Page, 2003, p. 1.
3. Graham Cray, 'Making disturbing sense of Generation Y', in Sara Savage, Sylvia
   Collins-Mayo, Bob Mayo with Graham Cray, *Making Sense of Generation Y*, Church
   House Publishing, 2006, p. 143.
4. Lindstrom and Seybold, *Brandchild*, p. 4.
5. Lindstrom and Seybold, *Brandchild*, p. 8.
6. www.tsa.uk.com. I am grateful to Jane Schofield of the TSA for allowing me a
   preview of the latest statistics in the report due to be published in 2007.
7. J. Coleman and J. Schofield, *Key Data of Adolescence*, TSA, 2005.
8. Safe on the Streets Research Team, *Still Running: Children on the streets in the UK*,
   Children's Society, 1999, p. 38. G. Rees and J. Lee, *Still Running II: Findings from
   the second national survey of young runaways*, Children's Society, 2005, pp. 7, 24.
9. www.childline.org.uk/AboutChildLine.asp, accessed in 2005.
10. *Truth Hurts: Report of the national inquiry into self-harm among young people*,
    Mental Health Foundation, 2006.
11. Social Trends No 36 2006, see www.statistics.gov.uk/downloads/theme_social/
    Social_Trends36/Social_Trends_36.pdf.

Chapter 4   Schools-based projects

1. *Mission-shaped Church*, GS 1523, Church House Publishing, 2004, p. 41.
2. *Mission-shaped Church*, p. 136.
3. Stuart Murray Williams, *The Church After Christendom*, Paternoster, 2005.
4. Arthur Schopenhauer, *The World as Will and Representation*, Dover, 1967, p. 45.
5. Time of our Lives was a youth event that happened in 1999 organized by the then
   Archbishhop of Canterbury Lord Carey. The idea was that each diocese in England
   should send 30 young people to London for a 48-hour conference and celebration.
6. See Robert Pelton, *Archbishop Romero: Martyr and prophet for the new millennium*,
   University of Scranton Press 2006, p. 73.

Chapter 5   Congregation-based projects

1. *Mission-shaped Church*, GS 1523, Church House Publishing, 2004, p. 75.
2. The drama hall at the Steyning Grammar School is fully equipped and hosts many
   plays and musicals. It has all the necessary lighting and latest video equipment built
   in which makes it an ideal venue for Eden.
3, Taken from the homepage of www.edenzone.com.
4. *Mission-shaped Church*, p. 79.
5. Richard Giles, *Re-pitching the Tent*, Canterbury Press, 2004; *Creating Uncommon
   Worship*, Canterbury Press, 2004.

6. Steven L. Case, *The Book of Uncommon Prayer*, Zondervan, 2002.

Chapter 8   Overview of the case studies: challenges and encouragements for the wider Church

1. I am aware this term is not universally agreed upon or defined, and that there are even those who argue that it should cease to be used of young people today. I am using it in a general sense, as a kind of catch-all for this generation of young people.

2. See, for example, Steven Croft (ed.), *The Future of the Parish System: Shaping the Church in the twenty-first century*, Church House Publishing, 2006. The fact that such senior church figures as the Archbishop of Canterbury and a couple more bishops, along with professors, theological college principals and numerous other impressively aligned experts see fit to contribute to the debate about the shape of the Church for these times gives a sense of the seriousness of the issue not just in mission with young people in the UK, but with mission with all the people in the UK.

3. Of course there is no catch-all definition for these umbrella terms. They are used by many different people of different projects, and mean as many different things. However there are some common strands; for further reading, see Michael Moynagh, *Emergingchurch.intro*, Monarch, 2004 and the Fresh Expressions web site.

4. The Universities and Colleges Christian Fellowship, Student Christian Movement and Youth With A Mission.

5. For example, Pete Ward argues in *Growing Up Evangelical* that the worship movements and trends of young people directly affect the whole Church within a decade. See Pete Ward, *Growing Up Evangelical*, SPCK, 1996; and Ward, *Selling Worship: How what we sing has changed the Church*, Authentic Media, 2005.

6. Sara Savage, Sylvia Collins-Mayo, Bob Mayo with Graham Cray, *Making Sense of Generation Y: The world view of 15- to 25-year-olds*, Church House Publishing, 2006.

Chapter 9   What might a youth-mission-shaped church look like?

1. Although it is important to retain distinctions – hence Colin Gunton's helpful reminder that the relationship of the Church to the Trinity is that of an echo rather than a direct correlation.

2. I am grateful to the Bishop of London, the Right Reverend and Right Honourable Richard Chartres, for this concept.

3. Dietrich Bonhoeffer, *Letters and Papers from Prison*, SCM Press, 1953.

4. Karl Barth, *The Epistle to the Romans*, Oxford University Press, 1968, p. 36.

5. Walter Brueggemann, *The Prophetic Imagination*, Augsburg Fortress, 2001, p. 66.

6. See in particular Eugene Peterson, *Christ Plays in Ten Thousand Places*, Hodder & Stoughton, 2005.

7. Susan Howatch, *Glamorous Powers*, Fawcett, 1989.
8. Graham Cray, *Postmodern Culture and Youth Discipleship: Commitment or looking cool?*, Grove Books, 1998.
9. For further information, see www.romanceacademy.org.

Postscript: What's emerging?

1. Margaret Withers, *Mission-shaped Children*, Church House Publishing, 2006, p. 121.

Index